STARR TRACKS
Belle and Pearl Starr

Belle Starr. (Courtesy Armand De Gregoris.)

STARR TRACKS
Belle and Pearl Starr

PHILLIP W. STEELE

PELICAN PUBLISHING COMPANY
GRETNA 1998

First printing, April 1989
Second printing, February 1992
Third printing, March 1998

Library of Congress Cataloging-in-Publication Data

Steele, Phillip W.
    Starr tracks: Belle and Pearl Starr / by Phillip W. Steele.
      p. cm.
    Bibliography: p.
    Includes index.
    ISBN 0-88289-723-3
    1. Starr, Belle, 1848-1889. 2. Reed, Rose Pearl, 1868-1925.
    3. Frontier and pioneer life – West (U.S.) 4. Outlaws – West (U.S.)
     – Biography. 5. West (U.S.) –   Biography. 6. Starr family.
I. Title.
F594.S8S73   1989
364.1'55'0924 – dc19
[B]
                                          88-3030
                                             CIP

Cover photo credits
Belle Starr, courtesy collection of Armand DeGregoris.
Pearl Starr, courtesy Hutton family collection.

Manufactured in the United States of America

Published by Pelican Publishing Company, Inc.
200 Newton Street, Gretna, Louisiana 70053

To:

Veleska Myra Ridley
Great-Granddaughter of Belle Starr

and

Flossie Mae Wiley
Great-great-granddaughter of Belle Starr

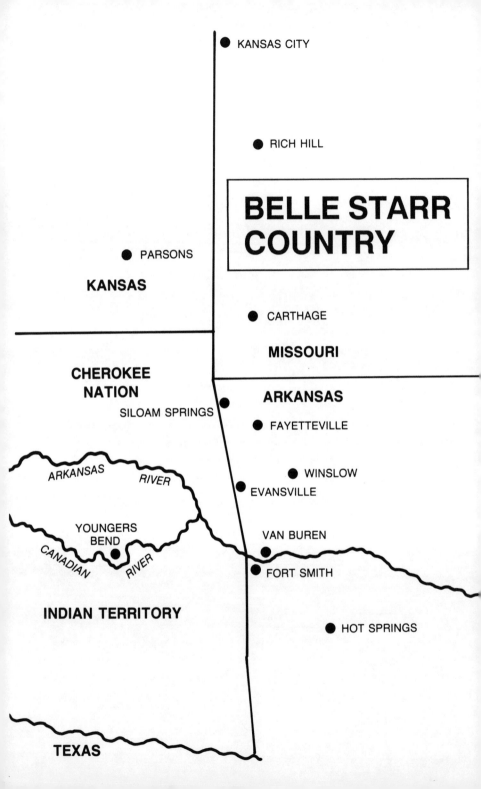

Contents

Pearl in her Fort Smith bordello.

Acknowledgments

As is the case with most personalities we know of from the volumes of literature about the American West, a great deal of fable and folklore has been written about Belle and Pearl Starr.

History recorded by the actual families of such personalities is often the best source for accuracy when attempting to separate facts from fiction. These recorded family histories have therefore been the basis for the preparation of this Starr history. The following descendants have not only openly shared their family records, but also provided the author with opinions, research assistance, guidance, inspiration, and encouragement. The results of their encouragement, as presented here, will therefore prove to be the most accurate and complete account ever written on the colorful lives of Belle Starr and her daughter Pearl.

Flossie Mae Wiley,
Colorado Springs, Colorado

Flossie is the granddaughter of Pearl Starr's first child, Flossie Pearl.

Veleska Myra Ridley
St. Louis, Missouri

Veleska is the daughter of Ruth Kaigler who was the daughter of Pearl Starr.

Charles Reed Young and Charles Benton Young
Little Rock, Arkansas

Charles Reed Young is the son of Mamie Reed who was a sister of James C. Reed who was Belle Starr's first husband.

Other than the above Starr family descendents, the following also greatly assisted the author in the research and preparation of this Starr history:

Brookie Craig,
Vinita, Oklahoma

Kenneth Butler,
Oklahoma City, Oklahoma

Walt James,
Elko, Nevada

Barbara Dew,
Librarian, Ottawa, Kansas

Guy Nichols,
Historian, Judge Parker's Court,
Fort Smith National Historic Site
Fort Smith, Arkansas

Tom Crowson,
Chief Ranger, Judge Parker's Court
Fort Smith National Historic Site
Fort Smith, Arkansas

Richard Miller,
Austin, Texas

Thomas E. Crofford,
Dallas, Texas

C.E. Miller,
Fort Worth, Texas

Preface

Few women in world history have inspired more books, magazine articles, and newspaper stories than Belle Starr. A full century after Belle was assassinated in 1889, still another volume on her life is presented here. One might therefore wonder what more can be said about Belle that has not already been covered many times by other writers. One might also wonder just why it is that this lady, given the title of "The Bandit Queen" by early newspaper writers, has attracted so much interest in the annals of American history and folklore. Certainly only three arrests and one conviction do not justify creation of the Belle Starr legend.

A somewhat plain and ordinary Missouri girl, Belle grew up in the heated political atmosphere of her father's tavern where Confederate sympathizers held spirited discussions concerning the approaching Civil War. Such an atmosphere, as well as the destruction the war brought to her home and former lifestyle, and the postwar injustice which fell on many ex-Confederates, no doubt contributed to creating the personality of Belle Starr.

Many such ex-Confederates, hardened and embittered by their defeat, found it difficult to adjust to postwar society. Roving bands of homeless men, many of whom secretly desired for the South to rise again, found their way to Texas after the war. Belle's parents, the John Shirleys, respected these young men for the cause they had fought so dearly for. Designated as outlaws, these men continued to rob, steal, and kill throughout the Southwest. Such men as Jesse and Frank James, the Younger brothers, the Fishers, Jim Reed, and others often took advantage of the hospitality John Shirley offered his Missouri friends at his Texas tavern and boardinghouse. Young Belle was living in an era of extreme turmoil, one in which her associations with desperate men began at an early age. Such an atmosphere further contributed, no doubt, to the development of a personality that was destined to become the legendary Belle Starr.

One must further consider the fact that little means of entertainment existed for 19th century farm families. Occasional barn dances, quilting bees, pie suppers, and church socials offered the depressed former Southern soldier the only escape from the drudgery of his daily survival. The dime novelists found great success and a wide market for their stories of bandits. Robberies of banks, railroads, and business establishments, which were often owned by Northern interests, were considered by most Confederate sympathizers to be a justifiable continuation of the Civil War. Ex-rebels, therefore, embraced such tales of Jesse James, the Youngers, the Daltons, and others. As writers' ink flowed in a volume sufficient to meet the requirements of an entertainment-starved society, there was little concern for truth or accuracy. Only the story and the sensationalism of the plot were needed to capitalize on the market. Writers, therefore, created many of the personalities who have now become American folk heroes and heroines. The honor of holding such a place in American folklore was not necessarily justified.

Such may be the case with Belle Starr. Early writers, constantly seeking material for their publishers' next deadline, no doubt saw great potential in the personality of this unique lady. Certainly her name was as romantic as that of Jesse James. Being female and associating in the rough world of outlawry normally reserved only for men, gave the dime novelist a totally new perspective. Thus a new leading character was created in Belle Starr.

Belle, who had always dreamed of becoming a famous stage star, greatly enjoyed the new popularity created for her by such writers. The personality that writers created for her in their stories, to some extent at least, forced Belle to live the part she played on the written pages of fiction. After all, the public expected no less. Belle, therefore, became a legend in her lifetime. So much pure folklore was created about her to sell a story that today it is often next to impossible to separate the true facts of Belle Starr's life from the volumes of fiction.

A few generally creditable biographies of Belle have been written. *Belle Starr and her Times* by Glenn Shirley; *Belle Starr and her Pearl* by Ed Hicks; *Two Starrs* by Robert Winn; *Belle Starr, the Bandit Queen* by William Yancey Shackleford; and many others are, for the most part, accurate and well written accounts of the so-called "Bandit Queen." Surprisingly, however, few writers realized that descendants of Belle and her daughter Pearl Starr are still living. Others may have realized it, but did not know where such family descendants might be located. History maintained within families normally provides the best sources for researching true biography and for separating facts from folklore.

Realizing that truth is often more interesting than fiction, this writer began a search for living descendants of Belle and Pearl Starr in 1983. Guy Nichols, a National Park Service historian at Fort Smith National Historic Site (Judge Parker's Court) in Fort Smith, Arkansas, provided initial leads. Photos left there in 1978 by Robert Hutton, who claimed to be a great-grandson of Belle Starr, indicated the man was living at the time in Ottawa, Kansas. No telephone listing for such a person could be found, so a letter was directed to the *Ottawa Herald*. The editor forwarded the letter to Barbara Dew, Director of the Ottawa Library. Ms. Dew then turned up the obituary of Robert Hutton, which explained that he was the son of Flossie Pearl Hutton, who was the daughter of Belle Starr's daughter Pearl.

Robert Hutton's only daughter, Flossie Mae Wiley, was listed as living in Colorado Springs, Colorado. A quick telephone call to Colorado Springs found Flossie. Not only was this great-granddaughter of Pearl Starr a most delightful lady, she was maintaining a large volume of material her grandmother had collected and written about Belle, Pearl, and their families. Flossie agreed with this writer that once and for all the true account, as recorded by the family, should be written. Flossie has therefore been of invaluable assistance in preparing this account of the Starrs.

Flossie further directed this writer to Elko, Nevada, where Pearl Starr's daughters, Jennette Scott and Ruth Robinson, had spent their last years. A trip to Elko resulted in many interviews there with old-timers who had known and respected Ruth and Jennette in Elko. Walt James, a seventy-six year old retired Montana and Nevada ranch foreman, had known Jennette and Ruth well, and was especially helpful in researching their lives and records in Elko. From this research and from obituary notices found in Elko, Jennette's daughter Delores and Ruth's daughter Veleska were found.

Veleska Myra Ridley of St. Louis, Missouri, who was born in 1912 and was seventy-four at the time this writer interviewed her, shared the concerns of her cousin Flossie Wiley. Veleska also felt that an attempt should be made to preserve their factual family history. "Too much legend has been created," was Veleska's comment, and she could not have been more helpful in providing family knowledge and photographs necessary for this new, yet old, tale of her great-grandmother Belle Starr, her grandmother Pearl Starr, and their families.

Veleska has no children. Jennette's only daughter, Delores, in Elko, Nevada, also has no children. The Belle Starr ancestry will, however, be proudly carried on through the four children and two grandchildren of Flossie Mae Wiley in Colorado.

This story of Belle and Pearl Starr, in large part, has come from the family records and recorded history of Belle Starr's descendants. As family members readily admit, over the past century a great deal of fabrication and pure folklore has shadowed the truth to such an extent that some lore has also found its way into family records. It is the intention of this writer, however, to present here the story of the two Starrs as they actually lived, and as their families and descendants have recorded their ancestry.

As indicated in the acknowledgments, numerous research assistants have contributed to making this work possible. Special gratitude must go to Flossie Wiley, Belle Starr's great-great-granddaughter, and to Veleska Ridley, Belle Starr's great-granddaughter for sharing their family documents. No doubt future accounts of Belle and Pearl Starr will be presented by other writers, as in the past. It is hoped, however, that the story of Belle and Pearl Starr presented here will not only meet with the approval of Starr descendants, but also provide a manual for future accuracy reference. I hope these true accounts also prove to be as interesting, if not more so, as those accounts presented by other respected writers who chose to incorporate the folklore sometimes necessary to hold the reader's interest.

Both Belle and Pearl Starr were showmen who dreamed of being recognized stars in the world of entertainment.

Neither accomplished that goal. On the stage of life, however, both played their parts well, and the Starrs will forever remain "stars" in the history of American society and
in the annals of American folklore.

*Miss Laura's Social Club in Fort Smith where Pearl Starr once worked. It is still
standing today.*

STARR TRACKS
Belle and Pearl Starr

Myra Maebelle Shirley (Belle Starr) around sixteen years old. (Courtesy Robert Hutton family.)

Part One
BELLE STARR

Tintype of Myra Maebelle Reed with her first husband, Jim Reed, in 1868. (Courtesy Charles Reed Young.)

CHAPTER 1

Belle's Early Years

THE SHIRLEYS

John Shirley, a native of Virginia, was born in 1794. He moved to Kentucky at an early age where he became a successful breeder of fine Kentucky horses. There he met Elizabeth Pennington, who was born in Louisville, Kentucky in 1816. Eliza, as she was called, was closely related to the Hatfield family which later became famous for their feud with the McCoys.

John and Eliza were married in Greene County, Indiana in 1837. Since John Shirley had a son, Preston, who was born in 1826, it is apparent that this was John's second marriage. Immediately after their marriage, the Shirleys moved to southern Missouri where they settled on a ranch near the community of Medoc (later named Georgia City) about ten miles from Carthage, Missouri. There John Shirley continued to raise his Kentucky horses and farmed along with the slaves he had brought to Missouri. John and Elizabeth had the following children in Missouri.

Charlotte A. Shirley
   Born: 1838
   Died: ?

John Allison Shirley
    Born: 1842
    Died: 1864

Myra Maebelle Shirley
    Born: February 5, 1848
    Died: February 3, 1889

Edwin Benton Shirley
    Born: 1850
    Died: 1866

Mansfield Shirley
    Born: 1852
    Died: 1867

Cravens Shirley
    Born: 1858
    Died: ?

John Shirley's son Preston married Mary A. Chelson of Iowa in 1847. Preston and Mary's children were Christian, born in 1848, and John, born in 1849. It is believed that Preston Shirley and his wife also lived near Carthage prior to settling in Palo Pinto County, Texas, shortly before the Civil War.

John Shirley soon became widely known and respected around the region, not only for his string of fine-blooded Kentucky horses, but also for his articulate political philosophy, which Confederate sympathizers around Carthage could identify with. Such respect gained John Shirley the title of "Judge" Shirley, which may have been first bestowed on him before he left Kentucky. Certain past writers have maintained that Judge Shirley was an attorney or at least a Justice of the Peace. No family or other records, however, indicate that his Judge title was anything more than an honorary one bestowed out of respect. Such titles were common for Kentucky gentlemen.

Elizabeth Shirley, referred to as Eliza or Liza by her friends, was also highly respected throughout the region. The envy of all the neighboring farm women for her talents as a seamstress, the beautiful dresses Eliza created rivaled any of the fashions of the period featured in the catalogues of each season's styles. Eliza had also brought with her to southern Missouri all of the Kentucky social graces she had learned as a child. Her social eloquence, and the fact that she was an accomplished pianist, made Eliza the most popular lady around the region.

Around 1858 Judge Shirley acquired a hotel and tavern on the town square in Carthage. Maintaining his horse ranch at Georgia City, he left his slaves there to look after his horses. He moved his family into the city where they took quarters in his hotel, which he named The Shirley House. Eliza's decorating of the hotel and tavern gave the establishment the air of a slightly second-rate Southern mansion. This elegance and the fine food prepared by Eliza and two of her slave women created somewhat of a culinary bliss that had not been previously available in Carthage. The Shirleys' hotel and tavern soon became the most popular establishment in the region and the favorite meeting place for circuit-riding lawyers, politicians, businessmen, and travelers on the Butterfield Overland Stage that stopped near the Shirley House on its route from Tipton, Missouri to San Francisco.

According to the family's ex-slave, Aunt Annie, the Shirleys' oldest daughter, Charlotte A., married a man named Thompson and moved to Matamoros, Mexico. She was still living at the time of Eliza Shirley's death in 1894.

John Allison, who the family referred to as Bud, was killed at age twenty-one in a Civil War guerrilla skirmish in southeastern Missouri.

Myra Maebelle, the Shirleys' third child, was called both Mae and Belle by the family. The Shirleys saw to it that all

Myra Maebelle Shirley around fourteen years old. (Courtesy Robert Hutton family.)

Belle Starr. (Courtesy Robert Winn.)

Elizabeth Pennington Shirley, mother of Belle Starr. (Courtesy Veleska Ridley.)

Cole Younger.

of their children were well educated and well trained in the social etiquette expected from an old Kentucky family. Belle, like her mother, had a natural talent for music, and she was given lessons in music, dance, and elocution at an early age. Belle's brilliance on the piano made her a very popular entertainer as a child. Not only was she in great demand as a pianist at weddings, church meetings, and barn dances, she also performed regularly in her father's tavern.

The Shirleys' fourth child, Edwin Benton, was somewhat of a problem child. John Shirley required Ed to help out with his horse ranch and with his livery stable in Carthage where he both sold horses and rented hacks. Ed, as did all of John's children, became an accomplished horseman at an early age. Ed was constantly in trouble, and was arrested and charged on many occasions for stealing horses. After moving to Texas with the rest of the family in 1864, Ed continued to be a horse thief. Texas records show that Ed was charged in horse theft cases there on May 3, 1866 and on October 24, 1866. He was shot and killed by a man named Palmer from Collin County in the Chamber Creek Bottom later that year. He was only sixteen years old at the time of his death.

It appears that the wild and daring spirit that moved men in the border states during this politically turbulent era prior to and during the Civil War greatly affected the personalities of all of the Shirley children. Their fifth child, Mansfield, was only fifteen when he was killed in a gunfight with law officers in Indian Territory in 1867.

The Shirleys' youngest child, Cravens, was referred to by the family as "Shug," and later as "Doc." Mystery surrounds this son. Although his name was originally Cravens, the family often referred to the boy as John Alva later on. Aunt Annie, the Shirleys' ex-slave, reported to the Dallas *Times-Herald* in her 1894 interview that this boy had not been seen for years, and that Mrs. Shirley assumed he was dead.

Growing up as a hotel child, Belle found she always had an audience. Lonely, child-loving strangers flattered her accomplishments, often beyond their worth. Others would tease Belle about her skinny figure and somewhat homely appearance until her sweet innocence turned into a rage. Belle's ill-controlled emotions, bringing on childish tantrums, provided further entertainment for the strangers in Shirley's Tavern.

By age fifteen, Belle had become a little more vain, greatly self-centered, headstrong, and theatrical. Described as not being pretty, but attractive, Belle's personality apparently gave her a magnetism men of this turbulent border country enjoyed. The hotel, the frontier atmosphere of the region, and her association with men from all walks of life around the tavern made Belle much more self-reliant than the average teenage girl of the day.

THE CIVIL WAR

Like her father, Belle greatly resented the Union movement toward destroying their family's way of life. The Shirleys were slave owners and depended on such help to maintain their farm, hotel, tavern, and livery stable enterprises. Most of their neighbors in southern Missouri shared their political views, and John Shirley's tavern became the center for Confederate activity in the region. A sharp-faced and beady-eyed young man, William Clarke Quantrill, had visited Shirley's tavern on several occasions, giving heated dissertations about the need to organize a Missouri army to fight for their beliefs. Young Belle, listening to such discussions, became a strong Confederate activist and encouraged young men to support Quantrill. Her older brother, John Allison, was one of the first to join Quantrill and became a captain in the ranks of these Missouri irregulars.

Belle, being a female, could not join Quantrill's men, but she wanted to help the cause in any way she possibly could. Quantrill needed information on federal troop movements within Missouri and other information. Belle, already somewhat of a privileged character in public places, knew everybody within 150 miles of Carthage as a result of their visits to the Shirleys' hotel and tavern. Keeping a sharp ear open around the hotel, Belle was very successful in picking up bits of information which she arranged to supply Quantrill's camps with. Although Judge Shirley strongly opposed his sixteen-year-old daughter riding through the night to carry information into Quantrill's camps, Belle was by now her own boss and apparently seasoned enough to handle any man who might cause trouble for her. Stories of Yankee soldiers stopping her horse, threatening to rape her in the woods, and Belle always somehow overcoming the enemy, were many.

Stories of Belle disguising herself as a man by wearing men's clothes and actually taking part in several Quantrill skirmishes with Union militia have been told by certain past writers. Such disguises used by Belle to protect herself from the rough young men in the field may have occurred, but any participation as a soldier in battle, however, is pure folklore. Quantrill would not have permitted any female to have joined his ranks in any manner.

Belle's brother sneaked home for a visit in February 1863. Belle was in Newtonia, Missouri at the time, some thirty-five miles away, when she learned that the Federals knew John was hiding out in the Shirley Hotel and were planning to capture him. Riding fast all night through the Missouri woods, Belle took many shortcuts while the Federal party seeking to capture John took the main roads. Few men could outride Belle. She arrived in Carthage before the Federals and helped John escape.

In the summer of 1864 John "Bud" Shirley and a few other Quantrill irregulars stopped at a Mrs. Stewart's house near Sarcoxie, Missouri. While there they were attacked by members of Company C, 15th Missouri Cavalry. In the fight Bud was mortally wounded. The next day Belle and her mother arrived at Mrs. Stewart's to claim the body. Belle had been very close to her brother. Regaining her composure after viewing his body, she was not timid in making it known that she meant to get revenge for her brother's death. One of Bud Shirley's associates, Milt Norris, apparently told Belle the soldier's name who had killed John. Shortly after returning to Carthage, Belle supposedly announced that she would marry the man who would track down and kill her brother's killer. Some writers have asserted that the reason Belle would later take Jim Reed as her first husband, in spite of her family's strong objections to her marrying the outlaw, was that Reed had killed the boy who killed Bud. Once again, there is no known basis of fact to this segment of Belle's life, and it must be considered as only more folklore.

In late summer of 1864 the Federals captured Carthage and proceeded to burn the city. The Shirley House was among the buildings that were razed by fire. Just when Judge Shirley had decided to leave Missouri with his family for Texas is not known. Apparently he realized the hopelessness of the war and the survival of Carthage and decided to leave for Texas only a short time before his hotel and tavern were destroyed.

Belle may well have been upset over leaving the country where Quantrill's young men were still generating a good deal of excitement, but as a dutiful daughter she went along to Texas with her family and several of the slaves. John Shirley first settled for a short period in Grapevine, Texas. In 1866 the family moved to Mesquite, and in 1867 they finally settled in the Scyene community in Dallas County. Scyene was only about ten miles east of the frontier town of Dallas, which would not begin as a major city until the railroad came there in 1872. Judge Shirley constructed a home for his family in Scyene, along with a tavern and boarding house. In 1868, Shirley acquired a 464-acre farm near Scyene. The Shirley tavern in Texas soon became a favorite gathering place for the many ex-Confederate refugees and the desperate, war-hardened young men the Shirleys had known in Missouri. No doubt greatly distressed over leaving her Missouri home and friends at first, Belle was soon to be pleasantly surprised by more neighborly relationships than the geography might have suggested.

TEXAS

Several groups of Quantrill's Missouri irregulars had drifted into north Texas during the war. Jesse James, who would later attain fame as an outlaw, parted with his brother Frank James in Arkansas during the war. Frank chose to follow Quantrill to Kentucky, while Jesse accompanied a group of men into Texas. Cole Younger also had occasion to visit north Texas during the war. At the war's end many of these war-hardened men found it difficult to accept defeat. Though many had returned to Missouri to surrender, they found the extreme hardships forced upon them by the Unionists unbearable. Forming small bands for protection, many such men became outlaws. Rationalizing to themselves that the war was not really over and that there was still hope for the South to rise again, such bands continued to plunder banks, railroads, and business enterprises owned by Northern interests. Many ex-Confederate families felt the activities of these outlaw bands were somewhat justified, and offered them food and protection whenever possible. Such was the feeling of Judge John Shirley and his family. Cole, Bob, and Jim Younger, Jesse and Frank James, and others were therefore welcomed at Judge Shirley's place in Texas. The

Belle and her third husband, Sam Starr.

Youngers even acquired property in Scyene and began preparing a home there for their mother and sister who had remained in Missouri. The women of the Younger family were suffering from the same harassment most other former Quantrill irregular families were experiencing.

Young Belle Shirley undoubtedly entertained a great many desperate war veterans and Confederate sympathizers at her father's new tavern in Texas. Basking in the admiration she had once enjoyed in Carthage from such men, Belle no longer missed Missouri. It was during this period that she may have developed an intimate relationship with the large and handsome Cole Younger. Although Cole always denied any love affair with his friend Judge Shirley's daughter when being interviewed later in life, most past writers recognized a close relationship between Belle and Cole during this postwar period. Certain writers have even gone so far as to credit Cole Younger with being the father of Belle's first child, Rose Pearl, who was born in 1868, although Belle was officially married to Jim Reed at the time. Cole Younger was often asked about this and his answer was always, "I have no children." The rumor of a romantic relationship between Cole and Belle and the possibility of Cole being the real father of Rose Pearl, no doubt comes from the fact that Belle would later name her Indian Territory home, Younger's Bend, and that Rose Pearl sometimes used the name of Younger instead of Reed. Belle obviously shared her father's strong admiration for Cole Younger and she may indeed have had a brief romantic encounter with him at some point. It is, however, recorded and believed by descendants of Belle and Pearl Starr that Jim Reed, Belle's first husband, was the father of Pearl.

Why Pearl began using the name Younger instead of Reed remains a mystery. Records of Judge Isaac Parker's federal court in Fort Smith show that she used the name

Edwin "Eddie" Reed, the only son of Belle Starr.

Mamie Reed (Young), Pearl's aunt who gave Pearl's first child, Flossie, to an orphanage in Wichita, Kansas.

Younger when she appeared before U.S. Commissioner James Brizzolara on February 22, 1889. She was also referred to as Pearl Younger when she was petitioned to testify in a horse stealing case against her mother in 1886. During the months Belle was imprisoned along with her husband, Sam Starr, in the Detroit House of Corrections in Michigan, Belle addressed all of her letters to Miss Pearl Younger.

Belle and Pearl's descendents' only explanation of Pearl's use of the Younger name is that Pearl began using it when her father, Jim Reed, became an outlaw and a wanted man. The name change may have been devised to protect Pearl's reputation. Secondly, as will be noted later, Belle had married Bruce Younger, a cousin to Cole Younger, in Kansas in 1880 before settling in Indian Territory. This marriage made Bruce Pearl's stepfather for a brief period, and Pearl could have begun using the Younger name at that time. Belle chose to name her Indian Territory home Younger's Bend, which was most likely in honor of Cole Younger, rather than Bruce Younger, since Cole had always had a close relationship with John Shirley and his family.

BELLE'S FIRST MARRIAGE TO JIM REED

Solomon Reed was born October 17, 1817, and died May 22, 1863. Solomon married a woman named Susan who was born May 6, 1821 and died March 18, 1900, but neither family records nor any of the living Reed descendants knew her last name. Solomon and Susan had the following children on their Missouri farm in the Metz community near Rich Hill, Missouri:

Francis Marion Reed
    Born: April 16, 1839
    Died: April 3, 1914

Margaret Ann Reed
    Born: February 24, 1840
    Died: September 14, 1916

William Scott Reed
    Born: January 17, 1841
    Died: December 2, 1869

Samuel Benton Reed
    Born: March 23, 1842
    Died: February 2, 1863

Teletha Larina Reed
    Born: August 9, 1843
    Died: October 18, 1915

James C. (Jim) Reed
    Born: February 6, 1845
    Died: August 6, 1874

Sarah A. Reed (Bush)
    Born: March 15, 1847
    Died: May 15, 1928

Jasper C. Reed
    Born: July 21, 1849
    Died: December 12, 1880

Solomon Lafe (Ed) Reed
    Born: December 26, 1851
    Died: August 26, 1922

Demanda J. Reed
    Born: October 6, 1855
    Died: ?

Henry Richard Reed
    Born: March 2, 1857
    Died: California (year unknown)

Mamie Reed (Young)
   Born: October 11, 1859
   Died: May 8, 1938

George W. Reed
   Born: October 11, 1859
   Died: Davis, Oklahoma (year unknown)

Fatima J. Reed (Jones)
   Born: October 7, 1863
   Died: ?

James C. (Jim) Reed joined the ranks of Quantrill's Missouri irregulars during the Civil War. This was the beginning of his association with Jesse and Frank James, the Youngers, the Fishers, and others who were to become outlaws. Since Rich Hill is only about sixty miles north of Carthage, and since Quantrill's men often visited Shirley's Tavern and Hotel, Jim Reed undoubtedly became acquainted with the Shirley family in Missouri.

In 1866, one of the Missouri parties of ex-Confederates drifted into north Texas and stopped in to partake of the hospitality Judge Shirley was known to offer others like them. Jim Reed, the Younger brothers, John and Jim Fisher, "Bloody Bill" Anderson, and possibly even Jesse and Frank James were with the party.

Belle's next actions has given many past writers a great deal of room for speculation. Although Belle was only eighteen years old and her parents strongly objected to her association with men like Jim Reed, Belle rode off with the party to Collin County, Texas, only twenty-four hours after they had arrived at the Shirley place. There a justice of the peace married Belle and Jim Reed in a horseback ceremony on November 1, 1866. Some writers have insinuated that Belle may have been pregnant at the time by Cole Younger, and since Cole refused to marry her, she chose Reed to be her husband and a quick ceremony was arranged. However, since Belle's first child, Rose Pearl, was not born until 1868, she could not have been pregnant when she married Reed.

Other writers have speculated that Belle married Reed so hurriedly because Reed may have been the person who avenged Bud Shirley's death during the war. As mentioned earlier, Belle had promised to marry the man who killed her brother's killer and was coaxed into fulfilling her promise by the party of young and desperate ex-Quantrill men she had so admired. Again, there is no factual basis for this assertion and it remains part of the Belle Starr folklore.

On learning of Belle's marriage, Judge and Mrs. Shirley were horrified. They immediately took Belle to Judge Shirley's son Preston's ranch in Palo Pinto County. There Belle was carefully guarded, and Jim Reed was advised to leave the territory. The Shirleys refused to recognize their daughter's questionable horseback marriage as being a legal and valid one. Reed soon learned where Belle was being held and rescued her. He then took Belle to his family home in Rich Hill, Missouri. Throughout 1867, a tug-of-war went on between Reed and Judge Shirley over Belle and finally her father went to Rich Hill and forced Belle to return to Texas with him. By that time, however, Belle's first child, who she named Rose Pearl Reed, had been born in Rich Hill in 1868. Belle and Pearl returned to Scyene where they lived with Belle's parents. Jim Reed had become a wanted man as a result of his participation with several known outlaw gangs.

Belle soon began frequenting the nearby boom town of Dallas. It wasn't long before she became quite popular as a saloon pianist and entertainer there. Often riding the ten miles home to Scyene late at night, Belle began wearing two pistols around her waist for protection. Sporting stylish velvet dresses and plumed hats as she rode sidesaddle through the streets of Dallas, her two pearl-handled revolvers around her waist, Belle created quite a spectacle.

A prominent Dallas medical doctor had made his objections well known concerning Belle's unusual dress and her frequenting saloons normally reserved for men. Belle, who considered herself a lady, became irate upon hearing of the doctor's comments. Seeing the doctor in his buggy on the streets of Dallas one day, Belle rode up to him, pulled out her pistol, and ordered the doctor to step out of the buggy to the front. This put the doctor between the buggy and the horse's rear. When a sizable crowd had gathered, Belle commanded the doctor to grab the horse's tail and raise it up high. "Now kiss what you see," Belle ordered him. With a revolver pointing at him, he had no choice but to obey. After the embarrassed man had done so, Belle issued a warning: "The next time you have complaints about me or my life style, doctor, make them to me." Then she turned and rode away, leaving a crowd hysterical with laughter. Needless to say, the doctor was never known to ridicule Belle again.

Cultivating a relationship with several Dallas businessmen, Belle was able to finance a Dallas livery stable business. With the knowledge of fine horses she had learned from her father, her stable became quite successful. Her husband Jim Reed was, at this time, associated with the Starr gang of horse thieves in Indian Territory. Indications are that during this period Belle was often provided with fine horses to sell by Reed.

THE SHANNON-FISHER FEUD

Jim Reed had become close friends with the Fisher brothers of Evansville, Arkansas, near the Indian Territory border, during the Civil War. Somewhat of a mountain feud between the Fisher and Shannon families of the region developed over a poker game. Jim Reed, Frank James, Cole Younger, and other former war friends of the Fishers were called in to assist the Fishers in their fight.

It all started when Maurice Shannon, the sixteen-year-old son of a well-to-do farmer, Granville Shannon, rode his father's favorite horse into Evansville. As he entered the saloon, the Fisher brothers enticed young Shannon into a poker game where they quickly relieved the boy of his money. In his final attempt to win back his losses, the boy then arranged for a $30 stake by putting up his father's horse and saddle. Once again losing to the Fishers, he told them he would need the horse to ride home, but would bring it to them the next day. The boy's father, Granville, became enraged after hearing the boy's story. Riding back to town, he found the Fishers, cursed them out for enticing his minor son into a poker game, and told them they would never get the horse. He also threatened to kill them if he ever heard of them getting his boy in a poker game again, and he warned Maurice to avoid going into Evansville. Young Shannon stayed away for only a few weeks. In February 1869 Maurice once again went to town. The Fishers noticed the boy, dragged him into the saloon, and stuck the barrel of a pistol into his mouth, demanding the $30 he owed them. At that moment, Fine Shannon, the boy's older brother entered, drew his gun, and fired. He killed Jim Fisher instantly.

Over the next several months the Fishers and Shannons found many occasions for gunfights. Four or five men on each side would lose their lives. One of the Fisher party to be killed was Scott Reed, Jim Reed's older brother. In August 1870 Jim Reed entered Evansville from Indian Territory. He found two members of the Shannon party in a general store and killed them both. From that point on, Jim Reed became a highly wanted man with hundreds of lawmen seeking the reward offered for him.

CHAPTER 2
The Birth of a Legend

BELLE IN CALIFORNIA

After the murder of the two Shannons, Jim Reed hid out in Indian Territory while Belle and her daughter Pearl remained on the Shirley ranch in Scyene. Hoping to escape the constant fear for his life in Indian Territory, Reed decided to take Belle and Pearl to California, where he hoped to start a new life with his family. Reed arranged for Belle and Pearl to travel by stagecoach while he rode out on horseback. Meeting in Los Angeles, for a while they enjoyed peace and happiness and lived an ordinary life free from the law.

In 1871, while in California, Belle and Jim Reed had a son. Belle named the boy Edwin, after her younger brother Edwin Benton Shirley, who was killed near Dallas in 1870 at the age of twenty.

Belle and Jim settled in the town of Los Nietos, located on the San Gabriel River to the east of Los Angeles. In a letter to Jim Reed's favorite brother, Marion, Belle describes Los Nietos as "an island," but since it is not an island, it is safe to assume it was a fertile farming area surrounded by rivers. Belle often commented throughout her life that the short time she was in California with Jim Reed and her children, Rose Pearl and Edwin, was the

Belle Starr.

happiest time of her life. The letter written to Marion Reed in Missouri clearly indicates that Belle was extremely happy in California. At the time it was written, she appeared to be planning on spending her life there. The letter, with all of its grammatical inconsistencies, reads as follows:

Los Nietos, California 1872

Dear Brother Marion,

I take my pen in hand to write you a few lines this morning. We are all enjoying the best of health. Indeed it is a rare thing for any one to be sick in this country. Marion we have received but two letters from home in a long time and they were old. Oh! so old I guess they had been written two or three months.

I presume you would like to hear how we have been getting along lately. When we left San Bernardino we rented a place in Los Nietos. Los Nietos is an island as is said to be best location in California. We then rented the place to a gentlemen [*sic*] by the name of Wolf. He gave us one hundred and thirty dollars for possession. Jimmie has bought land here on the island and I guess we will make a permanent home here. I am perfectly satisfied. I think in a few years we can have as lovely a place as this state can boast of. We don't care about if it never rains. We have the heart on raising everything we wish to as we have plenty of irrigating water. Jimmie is going to put out an orchard the first thing and then vineyard. You never seen such corn that grows here. It beats any land to produce ever seen.

Marion, Jimmie is very anxious for you to come here. He paid thirty dollars an acre for our land and he is compelled to raise $400 next month. It would confer a great favor on us if you could collect what is coming to us back there and come out here. Hays wrote to us that you had an idea of going to Texas. Do no such thing, come here Marion and if you don't like it you shall loose [sic] nothing by it. Jimmie is gathering corn and wanted me to write a letter and have it for him to take to the P.O. when he come in. Jimmie says tell you to make it in by Christmas any how. I want you to be sure and take dinner with us on Christmas day. I would not knowingly misrepresent things to you. Jimmie thinks you could do well here and we would both be pleased to have you come. Prest wrote that he was coming out here, but I guess it was more talk than anything else.

I have wrote to Manda, Sally, your ma, and Aunt Letty since I got a letter. I intend to quit writing. Do you blame me? Old Phillips (the old cuss) never considered to write us a line. Jimmie wrote him a severe letter last night. I guess he thinks Jimmie won't come back there soon. He might be disagreeably surprised someday when we get our land all paid for we will ask the world no else. Oh Marion an Orange grove is so pretty.

Rosie sends her love to all. I haven't written to Prest yet. She often talks of her doll Uncle Marion gave her. She knows her letters and can say the whole Alphabet. She has got a little set of dishes and three dolls. A ball and two hoops and a steel whistle. I will send Tima one of her little saucers. The baby is not very well. He is teething and looks very pale this morning. Write soon Marion and give us all the news. Give my love to all and I want them all to write soon and often. In haste.

MAY

Jim Reed wrote the following note on the bottom of his wife's letter (all misspellings have been left as is):

Marion I ritten to you some time ago and have not received any answer yet. I want you to rite as soon as

you git this and talk business. I have bought 47 acres
of land and I have one payment to make. The first of
in January which is $400 I have got $200 in hand and
stock that will bring it if I can git that. What is back
there Marion. This is a good country and I am shure
you can do well hear. The climate is good. I no you
can't help liking. This is good.[1]

The dreams Belle and Jim Reed had for their new
California home were soon to be shattered. Reed was recognized by California law-enforcement authorities, and
found it necessary to flee California for the safety of Indian Territory. Belle and her two children returned to
Texas by ship around Cape Horn.

Back in Texas Belle resumed her activity as a horse dealer and saloon entertainer around Dallas. Often riding into
Indian Territory for secret rendezvous with Reed, she first
met Cherokee leaders Sam and Tom Starr, who were
known horse thieves. In 1873 three masked men raided
the cabin of Walt Grayson, a wealthy Creek Indian who
had stolen a large sum of money from the Creek tribal
funds. The party tied ropes around the necks of Grayson
and his wife and threatened to hang them if they didn't tell
where they hid the $30,000 in gold. They raised and
lowered Grayson seven times and his wife three times until
they finally told where the gold was hidden. Jim Reed was
recognized as being one of the robbers. Soon after this
robbery, Belle Reed turned up in Dallas with a fine new
string of race horses. Since it was generally known that Jim
Reed was Belle's husband, stories were circulated around

---

1. The first letter found from Myra Maebelle and Jim Reed to Jim's
brother, F.M. (Marion) Reed was dated February 5, 1870 and mailed
from San Bernardino, California. The last letter found was mailed
from Waco, Texas on June 17, 1872. These Reed letters indicate that
Belle and Jim Reed were in California approximately two years.

Dallas about Belle, dressed like a man, also being with the party that robbed Grayson. Stories about the unusual woman who wore two pistols as she rode along Dallas streets were not uncommon, but it is doubtful Belle participated in such a robbery with her outlaw husband. There is no evidence to substantiate that she ever took part in *any* robbery for that matter. Tales of Belle being involved in robberies were purely folklore which Dallas citizens created about her, and they contributed to the trouble Belle began having in Dallas and around her home in Scyene. No evidence exists to indicate that Belle ever had any association with Jim Reed's illegal activities while in Dallas other than possibly sometimes selling horses of questionable ownership through her livery stable.

TROUBLE IN DALLAS

Jim Reed remained highly-sought after for the murder of the two Shannons in Arkansas and for the Walt Grayson robbery. On April 7, 1874, Jim Reed was once again recognized in a robbery, this time as one of the leaders of a gang that held up the San Antonio-Austin mail coach. Again, stories soon began circulating that Belle, dressed in men's attire, also participated with her husband in that robbery, but no evidence exists to support that story either.

Although Belle prided herself as being an honest businesswoman and a lady, the simple fact that she was the wife of one of the country's most sought-after outlaws began to cause her and the Shirley family a great many problems around the Dallas and Scyene communities. Belle's brother Edwin had been accused of horse theft, and was killed in a gunfight with lawmen in Dallas in 1870. Even Judge Shirley had been arrested without reason on several occasions, simply over the fact that his daughter was married to an outlaw and that men of questionable character often stayed at Shirley's boarding house in Scyene. As matters grew worse for Belle, she became irritated with the women neighbors who she suspected were responsible for the bad reputation created about her. She began writing threatening letters to these women, stating that if their bitter tongues did not quit she would see to it that some of her outlaw friends burned them out.

On April 28, 1875, a Dallas grand jury indicted Belle Reed for arson. Accusing Belle of burning a store owned by Nannie Reed, whom Belle had threatened on several occasions, a district judge named Barksdale set her bail at $2,500. This was felt to be a most unreasonable figure. Even a Dallas news reporter stated in his article about the incident that this sum was extremely excessive for these particular charges.

On August 12, 1875, the Dallas grand jury charged Belle and Mike McCommas with theft of a gelding and this time Belle was jailed. Stories of Belle encouraging the jailor to become her lover and run away with her have been told by past writers. Belle was released and soon after the embarrassed jailor returned to his wife but no longer with a job.

JIM REED KILLED

On August 6, 1874, Jim Reed was riding back to Indian Territory after a secret rendezvous with Belle in Dallas. John Morris, whom Reed trusted as a friend, was riding with him. Morris, desirous of the reward for Reed which was by now in excess of $5,000, carefully waited for the right opportunity to bring Reed down. As they neared a farmhouse in Paris, Texas, Morris suggested that they stop by for dinner and rest with the farmer, whom Morris knew. Explaining to Reed that Morris objected to firearms being brought into his home, Morris and Reed removed their gunbelts, hung them on their saddles, and entered the farmhouse. Morris pretended he was going to the well to get water for the farmer's wife. He returned to the house with his weapon, and shot and killed the unarmed Reed in the farmer's house.

Reed's body was taken to McKinney, Texas, where Morris hoped to collect the reward. Before the reward could be paid, however, authorities needed positive identification of Reed's body and sent for Belle. Arriving in McKinney, Belle looked at the body, then told Morris and the law authorities, "If you want the reward for Jim Reed, you will have to kill Jim Reed. This is not my husband." Obviously, the disappointed Morris did not receive the reward. Reed's body was buried in a potter's field near McKinney in an unmarked grave. A few months later Morris was killed by an unknown party.

On June 20, 1876, Belle stood trial on the arson charges. Pleading not guilty, that was the verdict since there was lack of sufficient evidence. The horse theft charges were also dropped in the same trial.

Concerned Dallas and Scyene citizens were determined, however, to run Belle Reed out of their midst, and they kept up their pressure on the authorities. In March 1875 a group of Scyene leaders formed a committee to seek ways of removing Belle and the outlaw friends who frequented the Shirleys' premises from their city. The following letter was sent to Texas Governor Richard Coke:

> Dear Governor Coke,
>
> For several years past the town of Scyene, Dallas Co., Texas, and vicinity, has been noted as a place of resort for horse thieves, desperadoes and other bad characters—certain parties having located themselves here as a place of rendezvous for such characters, thus giving aid and comfort to thieving and marauding bands infesting all parts of the state. Here is the

home of the widow and family of James Reed, the San
Antonio mail robber, his widow being no less cele-
brated in such exploits than her notorious paramour.
Here the robber and outlaw himself made his home
and sought refuge while resting from his daring and
infamous robberies and murders. Here Porter and
the Younger Brothers, whose names have since become synonymous of infamy throughout the length
and breadth of the land, for a time rested secure.
Here was murdered Colonel Nichols, a deputy sheriff
of this county, and Mr. McMahon, one of his posse,
while attempting to arrest Porter and John Younger.
Here, for a time, was the headquarters of the notorious desperado Hays, alias Parker, who shot off Judge
Hart's arm, and murdered in cold blood James Lov-
ing, a peaceable citizen of Dallas County. Here the
robber and desperado, Wilder, who now lies in prison
at Ft. Smith, rested while he concocted his infamous
plans.

For such characters the latch string of the home of
this family has ever hung out; and as courier, and if
need be coworker of the band, she (Mrs. Reed) has
done them good service. Donning often male attire,
she has ridden hundreds of miles to apprise them of
pending danger.

Quite recently she has threatened to burn out any
one who proposed to interfere with her nefarious
plans, and states, in a threatening letter to one of our
citizens, that she has twenty-five men who will do her
bidding and annihilate Scyene, if necessary.

Thus have they conducted themselves until they
have become a terror to the citizens of the county at
large, and the citizens of Scyene have been driven to
the necessity of organizing and banding themselves
together to aid each other in protecting their lives and
property, and to aid the officers of the law in arresting and bringing to justice all offenders against the
law, and by their vigilance to obtain and convey to the

proper authorities all infractions of the law, as well as to collect and present the evidence in such cases, thus aiding to bring to the bar of justice the parties who have so long preyed upon us.

In doing this, the citizens are desirous of being assured that they are doing nothing contrary to the laws of the state and that they have the sympathy of the officials of the state in what they consider a laudable undertaking.

With this view we, the undersigned, have been selected as a committee to confer with Your Excellency and ask your aid and advice. We have been led to adopt this course from a feeling sense of the responsibility resting upon us as good citizens and law-abiding men, having in view not only the good of the county, but of the whole state.

In Your Excellency's message to the Fourteenth Legislature, on pp. 15 to 18 inclusive, we have noticed certain recommendations in regards to such means as you deem most expedient to preserve the peace and quietude as well as the dignity of our state, which meets with our approbation. And, while we do not ask either pay or subsistence from the state, except in such actual expenditures as may be incurred in pursuing thieves and desperadoes for their capture and arrest, we desire the approbation of the executive of the state in our proceedings.

We propose to act only as law-abiding men and good citizens, and to go only where the laws of the land will protect us, and in no wise to take the law into our own hands.

Since our organization we have arrested and turned over to the proper authorities some half a dozen or more offenders, two of whom are charged with horse stealing.

We forward you herewith the certificate of our county officials, certifying to our standing as citizens of Dallas County, and ask that you take the matter into consideration and give us an early answer.

Governor Coke, certainly sympathetic to the community's plight but hampered by limited state resources, responded with a very noncommittal reply, reminding the group of the importance of staying within the law. A change in priorities from Indians to outlaws for the state police was still a few years away.

Belle's father, Judge Shirley, died on June 19, 1876. Eliza Shirley continued to live in Scyene until her financial resources were exhausted. For the last two years of her life she subsisted on the charity of the Floyd Street Methodist Episcopal Church congregation. At the time of her death on January 4, 1894, Eliza was living with Mrs. Charlotte T. Poyner at 636 Pacific Avenue in Dallas. All of her children, with the exception of her oldest daughter Charlotte, in Mexico, had preceded her in death. Eliza was buried in the Trinity Cemetery, later renamed Greenwood Cemetery, in Dallas.

Belle finally succumbed to the years of pressure and harassment of her family by her Texas neighbors. In late 1876 she left Scyene. Sending her two children, Pearl and Eddie, to live with their grandmother Reed in Missouri, Belle went to Kansas.

KANSAS AND BRUCE YOUNGER

Belle Reed was no stranger to the Kansas border towns of Galena, Parsons, Coffeeville, and others. She had traveled to Kansas on numerous occasions to buy and sell horses, and to attend occasional horse race events during the years she operated her stable in Dallas. Somewhat more financially independent from her property sales in Texas, Belle sought out the finest horses in Kansas and became a well known personality around the towns and tracks of that state. One of her horses became famous for winning most of the races in Kansas.

John Hargrove, a wealthy businessman from Siloam Springs, Arkansas, near the Indian Territory border, owned a horse that had never lost a race. As Belle Reed's Kansas mare became more and more famous on the circuit, pressure grew to see a match between Belle and Hargrove. Belle rode to Siloam, entered Hargrove's hardware store and challenged Hargrove's champion pony. They bet $500 on the race. News of the match between the region's best two horses spread rapidly and on race day hundreds flocked to Siloam Springs. Belle, seeking a way to fleece the wealthy Hargrove out of a larger stake, told her young Indian jockey to let Hargrove's horse win by a nose. Hargrove was not only richer by $500 when the race was over, but his horse was now worth a great deal more for beating Belle Reed's famous Kansas mare.

A few weeks later Belle again approached Hargrove and insisted on a rematch. This time, however, Belle asked that the stakes be $5,000 and the other's horse. Hargrove enthusiastically accepted Belle's offer. This time the crowds in Siloam Springs and the wagers made were even larger. Belle told her jockey this time to let her horse run full speed. As might be expected, Belle's mare left Hargrove's famous colt far behind in a cloud of dust. Hargrove had not only placed the $5,000 bet with Belle, but also placed several other wagers on the event. His loss to the cunning Belle Reed had also cost him his prize horse, which Belle rode proudly away with. The incident nearly bankrupted him and the method she used to fleece him made Hargrove give up the horse business.

Just when Belle met Bruce Younger is not known. Bruce was the eighth child of Charles and Parmelia Younger's nine children. He was also a first cousin to Cole Younger, with whom Belle had first been enamoured in Scyene, Texas. Born in St. Clair County, Missouri in 1853, he was five years younger than Belle.[2] Adeline Lee Younger, Bruce's oldest sister, married James Lewis Dalton, Jr., in 1851. Adeline and James Lewis were the parents of the Dalton boys who would later gain notoriety for their infamous attempt to rob two banks simultaneously in Coffeeville, Kansas in 1892. Bruce was therefore an uncle to the Dalton gang.

Labette County, Kansas, records confirm that Bruce Younger and Maebelle Reed were married by John P. Shields, a justice of the peace, in Chetopa, Kansas, on May 15, 1880.

This marriage, amazingly, would only last for three weeks. Cherokee tribal marriage records indicate that Belle married Sam Starr three weeks after her marriage to Bruce Younger. Little else is known of Bruce. Writers on the Younger family have reported that he did ride with various outlaw gangs. A newspaper report would later mention Bruce Younger's body being found in a New Mexico cave where it became mummified and was identified by one of Bruce's sisters, Sophia. The date of his death is not known. Thus, for a very brief time, Belle was actually a Younger and kin to the Daltons.

Belle was thirty-two when she married Bruce. Obviously somewhat vain about reporting her true age, the certificate confirming this marriage lists Belle's age as twenty-three. The reason for the brevity of Belle's marriage to Bruce remains a mystery. Three weeks later Belle left Kansas to make her home at the Starr ranch in Indian Territory, which she would name Younger's Bend. Most Starr writers credit Cole Younger, Belle's first lover, for

---

2. Marley Brant, a Younger family researcher, found information which indicates that Bruce Younger and James Lewis Dalton, Jr. were good friends and followed the race horse circuit together. Belle's brief marriage to Bruce made her an aunt to the Dalton children.

the name she chose for her new home, and not her second husband Bruce who was no longer with her at the time.

BELLE BECOMES A STARR

Belle married Sam Starr on June 5, 1880 in a Cherokee marriage ceremony, and moved into the Starr cabin. Soon after Belle had settled into her new home with Sam Starr, she went to Rich Hill, Missouri, to get Eddie and Pearl.

At last Belle had her family together again. With the Starrs providing support, in a somewhat questionable manner, Belle set out to improve her new home—cleaning up and redecorating the cabin, planting flowers, and improving the overall atmosphere of the place. This was a happy period in Belle's life. Located on a big bend in the Canadian River, some fifty miles west of Fort Smith, Arkansas, Belle named her new home Younger's Bend. Her children, Pearl and Eddie, would have been ages twelve and nine at this time. Myra Maebelle Shirley, Belle Reed, and Belle Younger, now became Belle Starr—hostess of Younger's Bend, which had a reputation of being an outlaws' den.

Belle quickly made friends with neighboring Indian Territory farmers, often playing piano for the region's church services, barn dances, and social affairs. The respect she once commanded during her youth in Carthage, and later in Dallas, was even more so in Indian Territory.

JUDGE PARKER ARRIVES

The Honorable Isaac C. Parker was appointed to the bench of Fort Smith's Federal Court for the Western District of Arkansas in 1875. With his appointment, Parker was given the responsibility of bringing law and order not only to western Arkansas, but throughout Indian Territory as well. His task would be a formidable one.

Situated on the southern bank of the Arkansas River, astride the Indian Territory border, Fort Smith was a bustling, boisterous river port on the edge of the frontier. Indians from many tribes and nations, forced to relocate by federal mandates, passed through there on their way to the territory set aside for them. Incidents of violent crimes, thefts, and other offenses were commonplace. The rampant crime that existed in this border country prior to Parker's appointment, as described by a Fort Smith news reporter, best illustrates what Parker found.

> "It is sickening to the heart to contemplate the increase of crime in the Indian Territory. It is time Congress took this matter in hand and organized a territory, for if crime continues to increase there so fast, a regiment of U. S. Marshals could not arrest all the murderers."

Treaties the United States government had made with the Cherokee Nation and other tribes when they were removed from their lands in the East on the infamous "Trail of Tears," gave the Indian nations the right to enforce their own laws within their own tribal governments. Indian governments had set up their own judicial systems with courts, sheriffs, and Indian police known as The Light Horse. Although these Indian law officials were somewhat effective in dealing with crimes between Indians, white citizens had been, for the most part, free of any lawmen in Indian Territory before Parker arrived in Fort Smith. The U.S. treaties provided that Indian governments had authority over all crimes between Indians, and crimes between Indians and whites who had chosen to be citizens of Indian Territory. Jurisdiction over crimes between white men in Indian Territory and crimes between Indians and whites who were not actual citizens, but only traveling through the territory, remained the responsibility of the

Judge Isaac C. Parker, "The Hanging Judge."

Parker's Court, Fort Smith National Historic Site, Fort Smith, Arkansas.

United States. These treaty rights were obviously quite ambiguous, and it was often difficult to determine just who was responsible for prosecuting criminals in Indian Territory. As a result, past Fort Smith federal judges had simply left the Indian nations' laws up to the tribal governments, and the territory became a haven for criminals seeking to flee beyond the jurisdiction of federal and state laws.

Determined to put a stop to this lawlessness, Judge Parker immediately organized one of the largest and best group of lawmen the nation ever had. Heavily-armed Deputy U.S. Marshals were sent out into Indian Territory with the assigned mission of bringing all lawbreakers into Fort Smith to face justice in Parker's court. Such aggressive law enforcement within their territory by the United States was looked upon by many leaders of Indian governments as direct violations of their treaty rights. Parker was well aware of these problems, but since the Indian governments had been so ineffective, he felt he had no other choice but for his court to take on the responsibility. Over the next twenty-one years Parker would hear three hundred forty-four capital cases. One hundred and sixty were convicted. Seventy-nine were hanged.

One hundred and three Deputy U.S. Marshals riding out of Parker's court were also to lose their lives during Parker's tenure on the federal bench in Fort Smith. Fear of Parker and his court soon earned him the nickname of "The Hanging Judge," and his gallows were dubbed "The Gates of Hell."

BELLE BECOMES A LEGEND

Belle arrived at Younger's Bend during the height of Parker's aggressive efforts to clean up the Indian Territory. Younger's Bend was already known as a familiar hangout for men of questionable character, and Belle was frequently visited by U.S. Marshals. Maintaining a delicate balance, Belle somehow commanded the respect of both the Starrs' many outlaw friends and some of the marshals. She was considered a close friend by many of the Fort Smith lawmen. Judge Parker himself highly respected her, although he was fully aware of the reputation her Younger's Bend home had for being an outlaws' den.

Belle had been a political activist since childhood. The pro-Confederate atmosphere she grew up in fostered strong beliefs within her. Being married to a Cherokee and having many Indian friends, Belle became a fighter for Indian rights. She accused Parker's men of often arresting Indians and bringing them in to hang simply because they were Indian. She was often found in Parker's courtroom seeking to defend such Indian criminals as Bluford "Blue" Duck, Jim French, Jack Spaniard, and others. Many times she paid expensive legal fees for those Indian renegades who had no funds for their own defense. Although Belle Starr was his adversary, Parker came to admire her for the concern and assistance she gave to many of her Indian outlaw friends.

Belle Reed, through her natural love for showmanship, had become a popular figure in Dallas during her sixteen years there. It was in Fort Smith, however, as Belle Starr, that she would become a legend. It was unusual for a female to be seen wearing pistols, especially when wearing them over the most expensive velvet dresses of the day. Belle Starr became the talk of the town and created a spectacle each time she rode sidesaddle on a fine horse down the streets of Fort Smith. It was the same response her appearance and actions had evoked in Dallas many years earlier. She was often being mentioned in newspaper articles about hiring lawyers to defend penniless Indian outlaws, and it is easy to understand how the dime novel writer saw the opportunity to create a new character in the literature of the American West. These novelists soon had Belle leading outlaw gangs throughout the nation, robbing stagecoaches, trains, and banks. The "Bandit Queen," as she was dubbed, no doubt made many a pulp writer a small fortune. Had Belle not enjoyed the new popularity such fiction writers created for her, she might have sued many a publisher for libel. Being the showman she was, however, Belle embellished such fictional stories which made her truly the star she had always wanted to be.

The Sebastian County Fair in Fort Smith played to a sold out crowd when the fair promoters talked the now-legendary Belle Starr into leading a fictitious outlaw gang in a mock stage robbery in the arena. One of the stage-coach passengers who stepped out to give Belle his watch and money at gunpoint, being none other than the "Hanging Judge" himself, created even more excitement for the crowds.

Unquestionably, Belle Starr lived and associated with known outlaws most of her life. She somehow found such men attractive. She treated all men equally, however. Whether outlaw, lawman, or honest businessman, she wanted to them all to be her friends. Women, for the most part, she detested. Belle considered herself to be a lady, and the comments made about her by women who condemned her lifestyle as shameful, brought out more rage in her than any encounter she ever had with an outlaw or lawman. Perhaps one of the original women's liberationists, Belle lived the life she enjoyed and detested most those women who tried to hide their true desires behind the social attitudes of the day.

Belle Starr with Bluford "Blue" Duck, a Cherokee outlaw she helped defend.

CHAPTER 3
The Final Years

BELLE CONVICTED

Belle Starr was arrested only three times in her life—once for arson—twice for horse stealing, surely not serious enough offenses to earn her the sobriquet of "The Bandit Queen." The charges against Belle in Dallas for horse theft were apparently dropped, and she was found not guilty of arson. Her only conviction came later, in Judge Parker's court.

On September 21, 1882, Belle and her husband Sam Starr were arrested when deputy marshals found stolen horses in their Younger's Bend stable. No doubt Belle and especially Sam Starr, had often been involved in stealing horses, but both claimed they had bought the horses not knowing they were stolen. Nevertheless, Judge Parker, perhaps influenced by Belle's reputation as the bandit leader the dime novelists had portrayed, found the Starrs guilty. Parker sentenced them to one year at the Detroit House of Correction on March 19, 1883.

Belle's son Eddie was sent to live with the Reeds in Missouri while Belle and Sam were in prison. Pearl was sent to live with a certain "Momma Mac" who lived close to Younger's Bend, in the community of Briartown, according to

Rose Pearl Reed (Pearl Starr). (Courtesy Veleska Ridley.)

research done by Pearl's daughter Flossie. Previous writers, however, have indicated that Pearl went to live in a hotel in Parsons, Kansas run by a McLaughlin family while her mother was in prison. Still further confusion arises on this point as a result of the letter Belle wrote to Pearl in February 1883, just before she was to leave for Detroit. The letter was addressed to Miss Pearl Younger in Oswego, Kansas. Since Flossie's research indicates Pearl stayed with Momma Mac at Briartown, this writer agrees with Belle Starr writer William Yancey Shackleford that Momma Mac may have been associated with the McLaughlin family who ran the hotel in Parsons, Kansas, and possibly had visited there with Pearl on a few occasions while Belle was in prison.

FLOSSIE PEARL IS BORN

Released in some nine months for good behavior, Belle—along with Sam, Pearl, and Eddie—once more returned to their Younger's Bend home. By now the territory was much more peaceful, and they settled down to be simple farmers. Belle, of course, continued to enjoy her reputation and often took trips into Fort Smith, leaving Pearl, now seventeen, at home with Eddie.

Belle had always adored her beautiful daughter Pearl. Belle dreamed of Pearl becoming the renowned stage star she herself had dreamed of being. Although Belle's attempts to train Pearl to play the piano had been useless, and Pearl failed to be successful as a child on stage in Dallas, Belle never gave up her dreams for her daughter. It is therefore understandable why Belle became enraged when she learned that her sweet and innocent Pearl was pregnant. Belle demanded to know who had done this awful thing to her daughter, but Pearl, apparently fearing for the boy's life, refused to tell. At once, Belle made plans for Pearl to marry a wealthy livery stable owner in Fort

Smith who had expressed a desire to marry Pearl on several occasions. Belle had always refused consent for the liveryman before since he was many years older than Pearl and she didn't think Pearl would be happy with him, despite his wealth. Now, however, since Pearl was pregnant, Belle felt a suitable husband should be found quickly.[3]

Pearl's secret lover at the time was a poor farmer's boy, Robert McClure, who had been Pearl's classmate at Younger's Bend school. Belle was well aware of Pearl's affection toward McClure, but she despised the McClure family. She also wanted Pearl to marry a wealthy man, not a penniless Indian Territory farm boy. Tired of Belle's constant pressure on her to marry the Fort Smith liveryman, Pearl left home and went to her grandmother Reed's home near Rich Hill, Missouri.

Pearl wrote to McClure, expressing a desire for him to come for her. Belle, suspecting such contact might be made, arranged to intercept all of Pearl's letters to McClure at the regional post office. McClure, filled with anxiety over Pearl leaving and not knowing of her whereabouts, pleaded constantly with Belle to let him know where Pearl was. Forging a letter in Pearl's handwriting, Belle wrote a letter to McClure explaining that, due to problems between their families, they could never have married and that she had married a wealthy man in Kansas. The angry and heartbroken McClure then married an Indian girl and left the territory.

Pearl, in the meantime, could not understand why the one she loved, the apparent father of her forthcoming child, never contacted her. Belle had written both Susan

---

3. Information about Robert McClure and the only known source to substantiate that he was the true father of Flossie Pearl comes from personal notes Flossie Pearl made based on conversations she had with her mother, Pearl, in 1924.

Reed and Pearl to the effect that she never wanted to see Pearl's child after it was born, and told her never to return with it.

Several past writers have had reason to believe that Pearl's first pregnancy was the result of an incestuous affair between Pearl and her brother, Eddie Reed. Pearl and Eddie had been separated most of their lives, and being left alone at Younger's Bend on many occasions while Belle was on trips to Fort Smith, such an illicit affair could have been possible. However, Pearl explicitly tells her first daughter in letters she would later write to her in 1924 that her father's name was Robert. These letters, only recently discovered in the family history records now owned by Pearl Starr's great-granddaughter, clearly establish for the first time that Robert McClure was the father of Pearl's first child.

A short time before Pearl gave birth, she and Susan Reed were escorted from Rich Hill to Siloam Springs, Arkansas by Marion Reed, Pearl's uncle. Mrs. Reed had gone there to take baths for her arthritic condition. While staying in a hotel near the springs, Pearl's daughter was born on April 22, 1887. This daughter was later named Flossie Pearl by her adopted parents. Pearl, however, gave her first child the name of Mamie after her favorite aunt, Mamie Reed Young, who lived in Wichita, Kansas.

Pearl returned to Rich Hill with her grandmother for a few months, then took baby Mamie to her Aunt Mamie Reed Young's home in Wichita. Belle wrote to Pearl there expressing a deep desire for her to return home, but further declared she did not want her to bring her child nor did she ever want to see it. Belle used further persuasion by telling Pearl her brother Eddie had been seriously wounded in a gunfight and longed to see his sister. Eddie was no doubt suffering, but his wound was not as serious as Belle's letter implied.

Pearl left baby Mamie with her aunt and returned to

Younger's Bend. Once again in her mother's grasp, Pearl was somehow convinced that it would be best for her child to be placed in an orphanage. Mamie Reed Young left the baby with a Wichita orphanage on November 19, 1888. This home arranged to find homes for babies in Kansas through a unique arrangement. Babies were left in various homes for a few weeks on a trial basis, and if the home decided to return the child, the lady from the orphanage known as "The Baby Lady" would come for the child and attempt to place it elsewhere. At age two baby Mamie was adopted by an older couple, Mr. and Mrs. David Epple, of Newton, Kansas, on February 19, 1889.

Epple was a German immigrant who had learned the shoemaking trade in Germany before coming to America at age eighteen. Traveling west on several jobs, Epple met and married his wife while living in Maryville, Missouri. Before finally settling in Newton, Epple established a stage line route between St. Joseph, Missouri and Calinda, Iowa, and it ran for several years. Epple later moved to Newton, where he was employed as the young city's street commissioner. Being childless, the Epples were delighted when the orphanage brought them the two-year-old baby. Although this child had been quite sickly and not wanted in previous foster homes she had been placed in, the love the Epples poured out to their new daughter soon restored her to health. Knowing nothing of the child's background, the Epples chose to name their new daughter Flossie Pearl, after two ladies in Newton they admired. Choosing the name Pearl for the child's middle name was purely coincidental, as they never knew their child's true mother was Pearl Reed.

SAM STARR KILLED

Sam and Belle were returning from Fort Smith on December 24, 1886, when they stopped by the home of their neighbor known as Aunt Lucy Surratt. A Christmas Eve barn dance was being held. While Belle joined the women, Sam joined several men who were sitting around a large open fire. A short time before, Frank West had been with a group of Indian lawmen who had captured Sam for stealing horses. Sam's horse was killed by the lawmen in the resulting shoot-out. Sam saw West with the men around the fire, drew his gun, and approached him. "Why did you have to kill my horse?" Starr asked. West denied he had done it, but at the same time he answered he drew his pistol. Sam shot West through the neck, and almost at the same moment, the charge from West's revolver struck Sam Starr in the heart. As West fell, he fired two more shots, one of which dangerously wounded a twelve-year-old boy named Fulsom. Both Starr and West died within a few minutes. Sam was buried in the old Starr cemetery near his Younger's Bend home. He was twenty-seven at the time of death.

BELLE'S LAST MARRIAGE

Soon afterward, Belle took Jim July as her fourth husband. July was only twenty-four at the time, making him fourteen years younger than Belle. July had been a friend of the Starrs and often hung around Younger's Bend. By now, the name Belle Starr had become famous, and under no circumstances was she going to change her name to Belle July. In fact, Belle was so proud of the Starr name she forced her new husband to change his name to Jim July Starr. Although no official record exists of Belle actually marrying July, some type of Indian wedding ceremony could have been performed. If not, common law marriages were quite acceptable under Cherokee law.

From all accounts this fourth and final marriage of Belle Starr was more like a mother and son relationship. Belle being so much older, treated July like a child and undoubtedly ordered him about. This had been Belle's nature with most of her husbands. Only Jim Reed seemed to know how to handle the spirited and domineering personality of Belle Starr. Although Reed was, by all accounts, a desperate killer and an outlaw most of his life, it appears that Belle was more devoted to him than to any of her husbands.

Belle's son Eddie Reed had continually caused trouble for her. Not only was Eddie greatly affected by the men of questionable character who frequented Younger's Bend, he also resented the affection Belle poured out to Pearl so abundantly. It appears that Belle and Eddie were in constant conflict, and it is easy to understand how the boy was destined for trouble. Accused of horse stealing and other minor crimes around the territory, Eddie got out of trouble by the use of Belle's influence. On each occasion Belle would give the boy a good tongue-lashing and threaten to disown him if he ever got in trouble again. Although Belle herself had stepped beyond the law on many occasions or stretched the law to meet her requirements for a livelihood, she expected her children to do otherwise. Both Pearl and Eddie were children of a man she once had deeply loved and respected. In her own way, she tried to influence her children to live within the law—although in Eddie's case it was sometimes almost impossible.

BELLE STARR MURDERED

On Saturday morning, February 2, 1889, Belle left her Younger's Bend home with Jim July, who was going to Fort Smith to testify in an old horse stealing charge against him. Belle had decided to ride along with her husband and stop by the King Creek store on the way to settle a bill for $75 which she owed there.

Saturday night Belle and July spent the night at the home of Belle's friend, Mrs. Richard Nail, on San Bois Creek some twenty miles east of the Whitefield community. The next morning, the two parted. July rode on toward Fort Smith and Belle to the King Creek store, where she arrived shortly before noon. After lunch with the store owner and his wife, Belle told them she was afraid of being killed by one of her enemies soon. She then asked for a pair of scissors. Removing a scarf from her neck, Belle cut the scarf and gave half to the merchant's wife as a keepsake.

Leaving the store at 1:30 P.M., Belle arrived around four o'clock at the home of Jackson Rowe, which was only a short distance from Younger's Bend. Mrs. Jerusha Barnes was also there and was cooking supper. Belle asked for a piece of Mrs. Barnes's sour cornbread. The Rowe home was a popular Sunday gathering place for the tenant farm families of the Hoyt Bottom along the Canadian River. Edgar Watson, Dick Hays, Mr. Enclang, Mr. Wilson, an Indian boy named Hare, Mr. and Mrs. Barnes, and others were at the Rowes' when Belle rode in. Watson, who lived only about 150 yards from the Rowes', and who did not get along with Belle, left immediately after she arrived.

Around 4:30 P.M. Belle left the Rowe place. The trail to Younger's Bend led around Edgar Watson's field and intersected the old river road near the corner of Watson's hog pen, some 300 yards from Watson's cabin. As Belle passed the fence corner and turned onto the river road which was filled with mud puddles from recent heavy rains, a shot rang out. Belle was hit in the back and neck and fell from her horse. As she tried to lift her head from the muddy ground, her assassin jumped the fence, walked up to her, and fired a second charge into the left side of her face. Thus on February 3, 1889, only two days from her forty-first birthday, Belle Starr was dead.

Site of Belle Starr's assassination near Younger's Bend. Belle fell from her horse on this spot after being shot in the back on February 3, 1889.

Closeup of Belle's original headstone with epitaph.

Original grave of Belle Starr. Souvenir hunters had chipped off pieces of the headstone which was later replaced and fenced off.

A few minutes after she fell, Milo Hoyt came riding up the road, and seeing Belle lying in the mud, did not dismount. He immediately started to Younger's Bend to inform Pearl of the tragedy. In the meantime, Belle's horse had apparently swum the river and come home. Noticing the riderless horse, Pearl expected trouble. She mounted Belle's horse and started back to look for her. Meeting Hoyt along the way, they then rushed to where Belle was lying on the trail.

Jim July Starr received a telegram in Fort Smith on Monday, February 4, and made the trip home in eight hours from the Poteau River crossing. When he arrived, he found that several neighbors had been doing some amateur investigations. Although suspicion had been directed toward Edgar A. Watson, no action was to be taken until after Belle's funeral.

BELLE'S FUNERAL

Belle's body was taken to Younger's Bend where neighboring women bathed the corpse and anointed it with turpentine and oil of cinnamon. The body was dressed in Belle's favorite black velvet apparel, and placed in a pine coffin lined with black shrouding trimmed in white lace. Her arms were crossed with one of her hands grasping the handle of her favorite revolver.

The funeral was held on Wednesday, February 6. There was no minister or eulogy spoken at the ceremony. Belle had often told Pearl that she wanted to be buried near her Younger's Bend cabin if anything ever happened to her. In accordance with her wishes, a grave was dug near the cabin. The coffin was carried to the grave and the lid was removed. Many neighbors, a few deputy marshals, and her many Cherokee friends passed by her coffin in single file. Each Cherokee dropped a small piece of cornbread into the casket, as was their custom in honoring their dead. The lid was then replaced and the coffin lowered into its grave where it was covered with large sandstone slabs in the shape of a roof. Joseph Dailey, a talented stonecutter in the region, prepared a white marble headstone to be placed on the west end of Belle's tomb. The stone featured a carved bell, star, and horse. Daily was not only a master stonecutter, but also a talented poet. He prepared the stone's most appropriate epitaph. It reads as follows:

BELLE STARR
Born in Carthage, Missouri
February 5, 1848
Died February 3, 1889

Shed not for her the bitter tear
Nor give the heart to vain regret,
Tis but the casket that lies here,
The gem that filled it sparkles yet.

As is the case with most graves of noted figures in American folklore, the marker was gradually chipped away by souvenir hunters over the years. What was left of the original stone was later removed and stored in the home of the property owner of the gravesite. This owner replaced the original stone with a concrete replica of it. Grave robbers long ago stole the gun buried with Belle. The remote gravesite is today somewhat better protected by fencing.

WHO KILLED BELLE STARR?

Neighbors investigating Belle's murder before Jim July Starr arrived home from Fort Smith all seemed to direct their suspicions toward Edgar Watson, the neighbor who lived just south of the Canadian River from Younger's Bend. Watson's tracks from his home to inside the fence where Belle was shot at the corner of his field were found. His tracks near Belle's body over the fence were also established. Two shell casings from Watson's rifle were also found in the vicinity of Watson's hog pen by which Belle rode.

Belle liked Ed Watson's wife and often picked up items for her when she went to Fort Smith. Belle purchased some red ticking material in Fort Smith for Mrs. Watson to use in making a featherbed. A piece of this red ticking was found near where Belle was shot, which further directed suspicion toward Watson.

Belle supposedly did not get along with Watson. She apparently had given Watson some of her better tongue-lashings on several occasions—the most noteworthy coming after Watson took one of Belle's letters out of the post office. Other writers have tried to credit Watson for the murder on the basis of the following story: Belle had learned from Watson's wife that Watson had been wanted on a murder charge in Florida before coming to Indian Territory. Belle then threatened to turn Watson in to the authorities if he caused her any more trouble. These writers theorised that Watson killed Belle to prevent her from disclosing his whereabouts.

Jim July Starr, finding Watson to be the most likely suspect in his wife's murder, forced Watson to go with him to Fort Smith where he would be charged with the crime. Watson stated at his hearing in Fort Smith that he was entirely innocent. He had been at his home with three other people when they all heard the shots. He then walked to the spot with them, which explained his tracks. The shell casings found in the vicinity from Watson's rifle were of no value, since it was proven Belle was killed from buckshot and not from a breach-loading rifle such as the one owned by Watson. Jim firmly believed, however, that Watson was guilty. He was reported as saying in the Fort

Smith *Weekly Elevator*, "In short, I think Watson killed Belle Starr, and I propose to use every effort in my power to prove it on him." Nevertheless, the evidence submitted was not sufficient to convict Edgar Watson, and he was released.

Watson had only come to the Younger's Bend vicinity some fourteen months before Belle's murder. Not being as well known, he was naturally the first suspect. Even before Belle's burial, however, it was being whispered that Jim July Starr himself may have been the assassin. His quick accusation of Watson and his determination to have him prosecuted when so little evidence was found, also made a few people suspect Jim.

After the ordeal Jim July Starr had put him through, Watson then directed suspicion toward his chief accuser. Jim claimed to have been in Fort Smith, sixty miles away, when Belle was killed, but his claim was never positively substantiated. Little has been written about Belle and Jim July Starr's relationship, other than the fact that Belle, being considerably older than him, treated him much like a child. She had somehow talked him into going into Fort Smith to answer the larceny charge against him. Answering to such a charge that might have resulted in a prison term may not have appealed to Jim, the more he thought about it. By this time, tired of the way Belle treated him, he could have followed her back home and waited on the trail to kill the wife who embarrassed him.

Robert Winn reports in his book, *Two Starrs*, that Milo Hoyt said Jim July had offered him two hundred dollars to kill Belle. When Hoyt refused, Jim replied, "Hell, I'll kill the old bag myself and spend the money for whiskey." Even Winn agrees, however, that this reported encounter between Hoyt and Jim July Starr is not documented, and is submitted here only as another bit of folklore surrounding Belle Starr's death. If Jim had actually been the guilty party, it is doubtful that he would have gone to so much trouble trying to get Watson convicted, nor would he have spent the rest of his days attempting to force a confession out of him. Also, since evidence indicates that Jim July kept the name Starr after Belle's death, he must have felt some affection for her and therefore would have no motive for killing her.

According to *Belle Starr, the Bandit Queen*, by William Yancey Shackleford, the trouble between Watson and July would continue over the next year. Watson was convicted of another crime somewhere in Arkansas and jailed. While trying to escape, he was shot and killed by prison guards. July, still under bond for his horse stealing charge, forfeited his bond on July 19, 1889, and fled into the Chickasaw Nation. Deputy U.S. Marshals Bob Hutchins and Bud Trainor caught up with him and shot him. A few days later, on January 26, 1890, Jim July Starr died in a Fort Smith hospital. He was 28 at the time of his death, and was buried in Fort Smith's Potter's Field.

Edwin P. Hicks, in his highly creditable book *Belle Starr and her Pearl*, draws a conclusion that it was neither Watson nor Jim July who killed Belle, but Jim Middleton, a brother of the noted outlaw John Middleton, who was a cousin of Belle's first husband, Jim Reed. Hicks asserts that John Middleton and Belle were having a regular affair while Belle was married to Sam Starr. Belle, Sam, and Pearl loaded up a wagon for a trip to Dardanelle, Arkansas in May 1885, where they were to spend a vacation. Middleton had been led to believe that Belle was in love with him and asked to come along on the trip. At some point along the way, Middleton assumed that he and Belle were to eliminate Sam. Fearing to ride through Fort Smith since they were both wanted by the law, Starr and Middleton left Belle and Pearl at the Poteau River. The men, being on horseback, were to take a longer but safer route around the city and meet Belle and Pearl beyond Fort Smith. Both Sam and Belle were aware that Middleton had been involved in a Seminole payroll robbery and suspected Middleton was carrying part of the loot taken there. Only Sam caught up with Belle and Pearl.

A few days later the stolen horse Middleton was riding was found tied along the banks of the Poteau River. The body of a man whose face had been shot away was found in a shallow grave nearby. Needless to say, John Middleton never was heard of again. John's younger brother, undoubtedly aware of the amorous persuasion Belle had applied to his brother John, suspected a plot by Belle and Sam to kill his brother, and thus had a reason to kill Belle Starr. This suspicion, however, lacks merit for several reasons. It is doubtful Jim Middleton would have waited so long to avenge his brother's death. Also, Belle was not with Sam and John Middleton when Middleton was killed. In this writer's opinion, Jim Middleton had little reason to murder Belle. True, Sam could have killed John Middleton over his affections toward Belle or for the payroll loot he may have been carrying. At any rate, Sam had been dead more than two years before Belle's assassination, and it is doubtful Jim Middleton would have risked being arrested for murder when no direct evidence implicating Belle existed.

Now for the final suspect. Author Robert Winn gives full credit to Belle's son, Eddie Reed, for killing his mother. Reviewing all the circumstances surrounding the other suspects, this writer also feels Eddie was most likely his mother's assassin.

The boy had been a continual source of irritation to Belle. It seems obvious that Belle, by sending Eddie away to be raised by his grandparents for so many years, was not close to her son. Furthermore Belle's sweet and beautiful daughter Pearl could do no wrong. Belle spent money on fine clothes, education, and all the refinements that were available on Pearl while the rebellious Eddie received only tongue-lashings and orders from his mother.

One evening, only a few days before Belle was killed, Eddie asked his mother if he could ride her prize horse to a barn dance. Apparently, like most teenage boys, Eddie felt he could impress some of the young girls at the dance by riding such a fine animal. Belle, on the other hand, had watched the way Eddie treated horses roughly and staunchly refused to let Eddie even near her horse.

Eddie disregarded his mother's orders, however, and rode the horse anyway. Fearing what Belle might do to him when he returned, he stayed away several days. Finally, when full of enough whiskey, he got up the courage to come home in the middle of the night. Jerking off his clothes as he stumbled into the cabin, Eddie fell across his bed in a drunken sleep. Belle arose and went to the barn, where she saw a lathered and abused horse. She then grabbed her riding whip and in a violent rage stormed into the cabin, yanked the cover from Eddie's nude body, and began lashing him mercilessly. The whipping severely injured the boy. Finally, crawling from the house, he got a horse and rode to a doctor's home in the region. The doctor, Jesse Mooney, Jr., was born in 1866 and died in 1915. He told his family the story of Eddie Reed coming to him in a very weak condition with deep wounds from a whip all over his body. Dr. Mooney also confided that Eddie said, "I'm going to kill her for this." This story was recorded by Dr. Mooney's son, Charles Mooney in his book, *Doctor in Belle Starr Country*.

No doubt, the true assassin of Belle Starr will never be known. It could have been by any of these four suspects or a number of others. From all accounts studied, it appears that Eddie Reed had suffered a great many years of bad treatment, leading to a growing hatred for his mother.

The whipping he took from Belle for riding the horse she allowed Pearl to ride but not he, could have been the final straw. It appears to have given him the motive for the act of violence that ended Belle Starr's life.

JUDGE PARKER HELPS EDDIE REED

Only three months after Belle Starr's death, Eddie Reed, along with Ed Lear, was arrested once again for stealing a horse in the Choctaw Nation. He was brought to Fort Smith and tried in Judge Parker's court. Although the evidence presented against him by the prosecutor was not sufficient for a conviction in a normal situation, and Pearl made sure her nineteen-year-old brother received the best possible defense, Parker apparently chose this opportunity to help Eddie.

As mentioned previously, Judge Parker, for whatever reason, had always admired Belle Starr and it appears Belle also respected him, despite the harsh sentences he often handed down to many of Belle's Indian Territory friends. Possibly recognizing that Eddie had the potential to be a good citizen if he could be somehow directed onto the right path in life, Parker undoubtedly felt the actions he took would be beneficial to Eddie's future. Overlooking the skimpy evidence against him, hardly sufficient for a conviction, Parker found Eddie guilty and sentenced him to seven years at the dreaded Columbus, Ohio penitentiary. He gave his associate, Ed Lear, only five years. Parker must have made prior arrangements with the warden at the penitentiary, explaining he only wanted to put the fear of God into the youth. Eddie was pardoned after serving only a few months of his sentence. He returned to Fort Smith and was appointed a Deputy U.S. Marshal by Judge Parker in 1893. It appears that Eddie performed his new duties as an officer of the law well.

In 1895 Eddie married Jennie Cochran, the daughter of Alec Cochran and a school teacher in Waggoner, Indian Territory. About a year later, Alec was poisoned by bad whiskey Joe Gibbs and J. W. Clark served in their saloon in the Claremore community. Hoping he would not live long enough to tell about being poisoned in their saloon and feeling his death would be attributed to exposure, Gibbs and Clark left Cochran to die in a garbage dump. Cochran lived long enough, however, to tell his son-in-law, Eddie Reed. On December 14, 1896, Eddie entered the Gibbs and Clark saloon with guns drawn, determined to close the place and arrest Gibbs and Clark for causing the death of his father-in-law. Eddie ran the owners out of their saloon. Gibbs and Clark armed themselves, returned, and killed Eddie with two shotgun blasts.

Eddie was buried in the Cochran family cemetery six miles southeast of Claremore, near the Catoosa community. He and Jennie had no children.

Pearl Starr.

Part Two
PEARL STARR

Pearl Starr (right) with two of her friends, believed to be bordello associates.

One of Pearl Starr's former houses in Fort Smith, now demolished. Note the star in the upper window surrounded by a string of pearls.

CHAPTER 4
Rose Pearl Reed

Belle Starr's daughter, Rose Pearl Reed, was twenty-one at the time of her mother's death on February 3, 1889. Although Belle had great dreams of her beloved daughter becoming a famous entertainer, Pearl's stage training was necessarily abandoned when a nervous disorder caused her to faint under the pressure of being in front of an audience. Belle spent a great deal of time and money trying to teach Pearl to play the piano, but Pearl sadly lacked the musical talent that Belle had possessed. Shortly after her mother's death, Pearl went to Fort Smith hoping to find employment.

Although Belle had made sure Pearl was trained in all the social graces required for ladies of the day, Pearl had few marketable skills. Also, there were few jobs for females in those days. Pearl, therefore, had little choice as to a means of livelihood. Being quite beautiful at that age, men found her attractive. She became a "lady of the evening" in a popular bordello in the river port of Van Buren, Arkansas, some ten miles down the Arkansas River from Fort Smith. Her training in the social graces, her beauty, and the professionalism inherited from her mother soon brought Pearl Reed fame and wealth.

Once she had acquired sufficient capital, Pearl left Van

Buren for the bustling city of Fort Smith. There she established her own place along the city's popular Front Street, also known as "The Row." The Row consisted of numerous gambling halls, restaurants, saloons, and bordellos along the river's edge near the steamboat docks. Judge Parker and his deputy marshals had, by this time, brought some degree of law and order to the border country and Indian Territory. Now safer for travelers going west, Fort Smith became a popular city for outfitting them on their western journeys. River traffic was also heavy, and the crowds of strangers flowing into Fort Smith made business there exceptionally good. Pearl had been constantly trained by her mother for the entertainment business. Although the type of entertainment business Pearl had chosen may not have been exactly what Belle had in mind for her, Pearl had little other choice for employment in this frontier city and so she made the most of it.

Capitalizing on the legend the dime novelists had created about her mother, Belle Starr, Pearl Reed changed her name to Pearl Starr when she moved to Fort Smith. Her place was distinguished by a bright red star surrounded by lighted pearls. Her parlor featured a talented piano player, the finest whiskey, and boasted "the most beautiful girls west of the Mississippi." As her business prospered, she bought other sporting houses, invested in saloons, and acquired considerable property around Fort Smith.

Pearl became pregnant with her second child by a Fort Smith businessman, Charles Kaigler. Although no official marriage record exists, Pearl claimed to have been married to Kaigler. On June 30, 1894, the couple's daughter, who they named Ruth, was born.

Apparently Pearl's relationship with Kaigler ended soon after Ruth's birth. A gentleman who claimed to be a count from Darmstadt Land in the German region of Hesse, somehow found his way to Fort Smith. Since he was a brilliant pianist, Pearl fell in love with Count Arthur E. Erbach and his music. Possibly because of Pearl's profession, the couple could not find a minister to marry them in Fort Smith. They therefore journeyed about sixty miles north to Fayetteville, Arkansas, where they were married by the Rev. N. M. Ragland of the First Christian Church on October 10, 1897. On returning to Fort Smith, she built a two-story home at 501 South 19th Street in a fashionable section of the city, known as the Fitzgerald addition. The stained glass window that adorned the second story, featuring a cut glass star surrounded by pearls, left no doubt as to who lived there. Naturally some of the neighboring ladies became quite disturbed over Pearl, the owner of bordellos, invading their neighborhood.

On August 24, 1898, the Erbachs' son, E. Erbach, was born. Count Erbach had become ill with typhomalaria and was placed in St. John's Hospital in Fort Smith before his son was born. Count Erbach died on September 13, 1898 and was buried in Fort Smith's Oak Cemetery. Their infant son lived less than one year. E. Erbach died July 27, 1899, and was buried alongside his father in Oak Cemetery.

This was undoubtedly an extremely depressing period for Pearl. She had hoped to make a break from the infamous "Row" and finally be accepted into Fort Smith society by getting married and moving into a fashionable residential area. However, her dreams were shattered with the sudden deaths of her husband and son. Pearl adored her daughter, Ruth, and just as her mother had wished only the best for her, Pearl had similar concerns for Ruth. To protect young Ruth from any ridicule that her mother's profession might bring, Pearl hired housekeepers to take care of her daughter in her 19th street home. She never let Ruth know about her enterprises on "The Row."

On May 5, 1902, Rose Pearl Erbach married Dell Andrews, a gambler. Pearl once more chose to journey north to Fayetteville, Arkansas to be married. Maurice Coffin performed the ceremony. It is interesting to note that both reported their residences as being Paris, Texas. This false statement and the fact that Pearl again chose Fayetteville to be married rather than Fort Smith is understandable. She was four months pregnant at the time of this marriage, and though she was a religious person in her own way, her profession precluded any contact with ministers in the city.

Pearl's third daughter, who she named Jennette Andrews, was born November 8, 1902. Fort Smith hospital records show Dell's profession as being a horse dealer.

Records of the Hiner and Hiner law firm indicate that Pearl filed a divorce petition and appeal for custody of Jennette in 1908. In her petition Pearl stated that Dell Andrews had abandoned her in August of 1904 without provocation, and left for Texas. She further charged that Andrews was a worthless kind of fellow who had never contributed to her support and had run through most of her assets during the two years they were together. Pearl further stated in these documents that Andrews was last heard of living in Flagstaff, Arizona.

As her daughters got older, Pearl constantly feared that her reputation as a notorious Fort Smith madam might harm them. Winslow, Arkansas, was a resort in the Boston Mountains, some forty miles north of Fort Smith. Pearl acquired a home there and hired a black couple as housekeepers. Pearl sent Ruth and Jennette to Winslow, where they were to attend school as Ruth Kaigler and Jennette Andrews, far removed from their mother's Fort Smith reputation and any ridicule over being the daughters of Pearl Starr. Pearl remained in Fort Smith where she continued to operate her row houses while dealing in real estate and other business enterprises around the city. Visiting her daughters by train as frequently as possible, she made sure they were the finest dressed children in the Winslow schools. They were also given lessons in music and all the other cultural training available in the town.

Although Pearl, like her mother, had been raised in the midst of known outlaws, Pearl Starr was never known to have been involved with illegal activities around Fort Smith. The only time she was ever implicated in a crime was in the spring of 1911. A group of men burglarized the Stockburger, Miller and Co. general merchandise store in Winslow. Local lawmen investigating the crime found several items of clothing, expensive coats, and bolts of material taken in the robbery hidden at Pearl's Winslow home.

The next day City Marshal Dan Murphy arrested Pearl as she arrived by train to see her daughters. Taken to Fayetteville and charged with the crime, Pearl posted bond and returned to Fort Smith. The gang involved in the robbery, finding a posse close on their heels, could not carry all the stolen items and somehow had used Pearl's Winslow home to stash them. The men escaped over the Arkansas state line but were later apprehended in Fort Smith.

Pearl hired the Fort Smith law firm of Hiner and Hiner for her defense. The jury, without question influenced by the fact that Pearl was the daughter of the notorious bandit queen, Belle Starr, and the operator of an irreputable Fort Smith enterprise, found Pearl guilty after hearing the testimony. She was sentenced to one year in the Arkansas State Penitentiary. Posting $2,000 bail, Pearl's attorneys appealed the verdict to the Arkansas Supreme Court which overturned it, stating that the Fayetteville court had erred.

Pearl's honest dealings and pleasant personality made her quite popular with the Fort Smith business community. Although the nature of her bordello business was considered damaging to the city's reputation, Pearl enjoyed a good relationship with most of the city's leaders and the police department throughout her years in Fort Smith. However, women's clubs and church groups began putting pressure on city officials to clean up "The Row." Around 1916 these pressures resulted in the enactment of municipal ordinances making prostitution illegal in the city. For a few years Pearl Starr's place was overlooked as she continued to operate, but eventually she was arrested for her illegal operations. Since she had many friends among the city officials the charges were dropped, but there was an understanding that she would leave their community—no doubt to the regret of her many clients and business associates in Fort Smith.

Pearl sold her homes and properties in Fort Smith and Winslow and moved to Bisbee, Arizona. There she operated the Starr Hotel and invested in a copper mine. Later she would also acquire a boarding house known as the Savoy Hotel in Douglas, Arizona.

Jennette Andrews Scott.

Veleska Myra Walt Ridley, daughter of Ruth Kaigler Walt.

CHAPTER 5

Pearl's Daughters and Other Starr Descendents

MAMIE (FLOSSIE PEARL EPPLE HUTTON)

Pearl was approximately fifty-three years of age when she left Fort Smith for Arizona. She had not heard from nor been in contact with her first daughter, Flossie Pearl, since leaving the child with her Aunt Mamie shortly after Flossie's birth in 1887. Jim Reed's sister, Mamie Reed (Young), fearing what Belle might do if she kept the child, took Flossie to an orphanage in Wichita, Kansas and left her there.

As mentioned earlier, Pearl had originally named the baby Mamie, but after she was adopted at the age of two by David Epple and his wife, they renamed her Flossie Pearl. The Epples raised Flossie in the town of Newton, Kansas. As the street commissioner in that city, Epple was able to give Flossie the best possible education, and she apparently developed her natural talent as a writer and journalist. Flossie married her childhood sweetheart, Charles Hutton, on May 14, 1907. Charles was employed by the railroad in Newton. Charles and Flossie had one child, Robert E. Hutton, born August 27, 1908 in Newton.

Pearl Starr, the real mother Flossie had never known, wanted to see her first child again before she died, and she directed a letter to the orphanage where Flossie had been left as an infant. The orphanage sent it to Mrs. Epple, who was no longer living. Flossie found the letter, and for the first time she learned about her family heritage and who her real mother was. Flossie immediately replied to Pearl, explaining that she must be the child she was seeking and looked forward to hearing further from Pearl regarding her background. Pearl's emotion-filled reply to Flossie is as follows.

Dearest Child:

Your letter received and their [sic] is no doubt in my mind about you not being the same baby. But my mother signed my name to those papers which you have. Always rememmber [sic] that your mother did not sign those papers. For I would never have done that. But through a missunderstanding [sic] you were taken from me. My aunt that lived in Wichita is such a good woman, and she told me you were with people that loved you so much. But she had pledged her word to never tell where you were, and she never did. I always write to her on your birthday, and remind her that I am thinking of you. You will be thirty eight years old April 22, 1925. You were born April 22, 1887. You were sixteen months old when I last saw you. I can see yet how you looked. You were such a pretty baby. You had the bluest eyes. You didn't have so much hair, but it was brown and of a pretty shade. And you had such small hands and feet. I loved you with all my heart.

I have some of your little things and a baby picture, and many times I kissed them before going to sleep. I am happy to know that you have a good husband and a nice boy. I am sure that you are happy. That is one thing that I always wanted to know—how you were getting along. And now that I had the pleasure of reading a nice letter from you my mind will be at ease.

And someday, as you say, we may meet again. I will love the memmory [*sic*] of Mr. and Mrs. Epple for their kind treatment to you. I am glad you appreciated all that they did for you.

You have two sisters. One is seven years younger than you and the other is fourteen years younger. The oldest one is married, and has a lovely little girl. They both play the piano. I am so glad that you play, for we all love music.

Please send me a picture of yourself and family. So now I will close with love to you and yours.

Your mother,

Mrs. Rosa. Reed

P.S. Look over mistakes for I have been crying. I can't say just how I feel—I just couldn't make you understand how I do feel. Let me hear from you, dear— bye-bye.

Flossie's next letter to Pearl, who had chosen to use the name of Rosa Reed in Arizona, talked about her son, Robert Hutton, whom they called Bob. Flossie said that she hoped to soon be able to go to Arizona for a long overdue reunion with her mother, and she would be bringing Bob to meet his grandmother. Pearl's second reply is as follows:

Dearest Daughter:

Your letter received and more than pleased to hear from you. So many things I want to say that I hardly know what to say first. But some day maybe I will see you then I can explain everything. You see, I loved my mother dearly. But she didn't want me to marry your father, and I ran away and married him. She wouldn't let me live with him. She separated us and he went away. Later she discovered that I was going to have a baby. She had wanted me to marry a rich man that was in love with me, but I didn't want him. I

Flossie Pearl Hutton (left) with son, Robert Hutton, at their first meeting with Pearl Starr in Arizona, 1924.

loved your father dearly. I went to school with him and always loved him. He went away and was going to send for me. I lived on a ranch in the Indian Territory and it was a long ways to the Post Office. My mother got the mail and so I didn't hear from him. So I ran away from home. I went to Missouri to Grandma Reeds and asked her not to let my mother know I was there.

I stayed with my dear old grandma until you were here and two months old. Then I went to Wichita, Kansas to live with Aunt Mammie [*sic*]. I named you Mamie after her. I lived with her till you were one year old. Then my mother found out I was there and I went to Missouri to Grandma's. I stayed there till you were sixteen months old.

I only had one brother and no sisters. My brother got sick and they didn't think he could live. He kept calling for me. My mother sent for me to come home at once. I took you in my arms and cryed [*sic*] all night. I got a cousin to come and stay with Grandma to look after you. I went home. I had to ride horseback thirty-four miles after getting off the train. The weather was warm. You wer'n't [*sic*] very well and were cutting teeth, I had never been away from you a whole day in your life.

I got home and my brother was getting better. They treated me lovely. When I was there four days I told my mother that I was going back to Missouri and that I couldn't stay away from my baby any longer. Then she told me that I WAS NOT going back. She made many threats. I wrote to my aunt Mamie in Wichita and asked her to go and get you and keep you until I could get away from my mother. I told her that I would come as soon as I could. I gave the letter to a ranch hand to mail. My mother maid [*sic*] him give it to her and she read it. Then she wrote my Aunt Mamie and threatened her. So my dear aunt Mamie that loved you dearly took you to the Children's

Home. They sent some papers to be signed and my mother wanted me to sign them. But I would never sign a paper to give one of my children away. I ran screaming from the house without looking at the paper. I went to Aunt Mamie and she would never tell me anything. She told me that she had pledged her word and couldn't. She told me that they called you Flossie, and that they loved you dearly. She told me that I would have to go to the courts and get you.

Did you ever know Mrs. Dr. Stoner? Aunt Mamie told me that they were good friends to the people that had taken you. But she wouldn't tell me their names and told me that she didn't know where they lived. So you see, I didn't know how to find you.

I always write aunt Mamie on your birthday. She is still living, and I hope someday that we can visit her together. She has one of the pictures like I am sending you, when you were five months old. The little picture looks dim, for I have kissed the little face so many times. I have one that is enlarged and will send you the little one.

You said you wrote me on dear Bob's birthday. And Flossie you will be surprised when I tell you that your father's name was Robert, and that we called him Bob. We talked about you many times. He has been dead for many years.

Your sisters are half sisters, and I have always told them that they had a sister, WE have always talked about you, and sometimes they ask me so many questions. You see I felt so bad to explain everything. I hated to talk about my mother and tell how she had made me lose my baby. But thank the good Lord you were with those that loved you. And you didn't know and worry about a poor little mamma that couldn't sleep for crying and thinking of you.

I was a very sickly young woman, but now my health is very good. I am sorry you are not well.

No, we won't have any publicity. I am only glad to know that my dear little Mamie is happy, for I loved you so much. And to be punished so for marrying a man I loved and bringing a nice baby into the world! I can't understand it; and my mother caused it all. She had only one thought, and that I must not marry a poor man.

You asked me to write you a letter a mile long and it seems like I am going to do it. I guess this all seems stranged [sic] to you. I always felt that someday I would find you. Look over my mistakes. It always hurts me to think back over the years and review all I have told you. I love you just as much as I do your sisters and from your letters you are a wonderful woman in my estimation. I am sure Mrs. Epple was never ashamed of you. As I told you before I will always love their memmory [sic] for being so good to you. I love everyone that has ever crossed your path that has been good to you.

I will send you some pictures soon, and your sisters will write you. Remember me kindly to your husband and Bob. I love him even if I've never saw him. To think I have a grandson!

Now read my letter and remember when I was a girl the country wasn't like it is now. We didn't have telephones and autos and so many railroads. I lived away out on a ranch and not close to anyone. So you can see my lot was not always an easy one.

Now I will close. Let me hear from you soon.

With lots of love,
Your *OWN* Mother.

Pearl's second letter to Flossie leaves little doubt that the true father of Flossie was none other than Pearl's classmate and lover, Robert McClure. The statement Pearl makes about running away and marrying Flossie's father is not believed to be true. Naturally, Pearl felt somewhat guilty for having Flossie out of wedlock and no doubt made this statement to give her daughter a better feeling about her mother. As mentioned earlier, many past writers have insinuated that Flossie's true father was Pearl's brother, Eddie Reed—or half-brother if the Cole Younger story of being Pearl's father is to be believed. However, this second letter Pearl wrote to her daughter Flossie when Flossie was thirty-seven proves that Eddie Reed was not Flossie's father.

In 1924, one year before Pearl died, Flossie and her son, Robert Hutton, went to Arizona to meet Pearl for the first time. Pearl died in Douglas, Arizona on July 6, 1925 at the age of fifty-seven. There she is buried as Rose Pearl Reed. Her daughters apparently chose not to use the better-known Pearl Starr name to prevent souvenir hunters from desecrating Pearl's headstone.

After meeting her real mother and learning of her Belle Starr heritage, Flossie became an avid researcher and writer on Starr history. She had many articles published in various newspapers throughout the nation, and was in the process of writing a book about her family and background when she died in 1943. The original research and direct interviews Flossie had with her mother have been invaluable in the preparation of this Starr history.

Flossie, like her grandmother Belle, had always been concerned with the plight of the American Indian and she chose to help Indian families throughout her lifetime. Spending vacations in Hot Springs, Arkansas, Flossie met an Apache named Altaha Gomechez Greyhorse, who claimed to have been related to the great Apache Chief, Cochise. Greyhorse was working in Hot Springs for the operators of various tourist hotels where he was paid to give lectures on Indian culture and to perform Indian dances. Noting Greyhorse's children, Nepanee and Bonito, needed assistance, Flossie arranged for them to be enrolled in the Bacone Indian School in Muskogee, Oklahoma. There Flossie saw to their proper educations and support. Nepanee Goforth, now married to a dairy farmer near Siloam Springs, Arkansas, and her brother Bonito Greyhorse, associated with American Airlines in Tulsa, Oklahoma, are forever grateful to the help and assistance Flossie Pearl Hutton provided them during their early lives.

Flossie's son, Robert Hutton, born August 27, 1908, married Grace Lucille Kennedy on June 2, 1927. They were divorced on July 1, 1936, and he later married Rheva Wright Mack. Robert and Grace had one daughter, who proudly bears the names of her grandmother, Flossie Pearl Hutton, and great-great-grandmother Belle Starr. Flossie Mae Hutton was born December 27, 1927. Her father, Robert Hutton, died June 24, 1978, and his first wife Grace, on August 8, 1984. Flossie married Jack O. Wiley on June 19, 1945, and they now reside in Colorado. Their children and grandchildren, the last descendants of Belle and Pearl Starr, are as follows:

> Bette Lou Wiley
> > Born: April 17, 1947
> > Married: William R. Good, November 26, 1965
> > > Born: April 5, 1944
> > Children: Lauralee Good (born April 12, 1966)
> > > Married: James Hitchens, 1987
> > > William Russell Good (born February 21, 1969)
> > > Jackson Robert Good (born May 27, 1972)
>
> Robert Lee Wiley
> > Born: October 19, 1948
> > Married: Janet Sue Latham, August 13, 1977
> > > Born: September 7, 1956
>
> Frank William Wiley
> > Born: October 5, 1950

Pearl Starr and her daughter, Ruth Kaigler.

Married: Deborah Jean Anders, June 4, 1971
    Born: October 24, 1950
Children: Rockie Lee Wiley (born September 4, 1972)

Flossie Pearl Hutton died in Topeka, Kansas, August 7, 1943, and was buried in the Newton, Kansas cemetery.

RUTH D. KAIGLER

Pearl's daughter Ruth was 27 when her mother left for Arizona. Before leaving, Pearl arranged for Ruth to be enrolled in the Strassberger Music Conservatory in St. Louis, Missouri. There Ruth met Ralph Walt from Ohio who was also a student there. They were married September 20, 1911. They moved back to Fort Smith for a short while where Ruth's father, Charles Kaigler, was living. While in Fort Smith their daughter Veleska Myra Walt was born November 1, 1912. They returned to St. Louis where Ralph Walt was employed by the railroad.

Ruth, apparently inheriting some of her grandmother Belle's restless spirit, left her husband and daughter when Veleska was eleven. Ruth then married a musician, Edward Drewitt, and traveled with him and his orchestra. Drewitt died while playing an engagement in Louisiana. Ruth then went to see her mother, Pearl, in Arizona and stayed there awhile before going to California. She met another musician, Roy "Deke" Robinson, in California. The Robinsons were both excellent musicians and were popular entertainers in supper clubs and hotels for many years on the West Coast. Deke Robinson died while playing an engagement in San Luis Obispo, California. A short time later, Ruth moved to Elko, Nevada, where her half-sister Jennette was living. Ruth entertained in Jennette's hotels and casinos around Elko until her death in 1979.

Veleska first married John Campbell in St. Louis on January 1, 1935. Campbell died December 25, 1953. Veleska then married Ernest Ridley January 14, 1954. Ridley was employed as a security guard with Washington University in St. Louis, and he died January 13, 1973. Veleska had no children from either marriage.

Veleska was still living in St. Louis at age 74 when this writer interviewed her. She said she is also extremely proud of her Belle and Pearl Starr ancestry, but was not aware of it until she was thirty-one years of age. Her father asked her to go to a movie with him. The picture they saw was the 1941 film, "Belle Starr," which starred Gene Tierney. The film was made in Pineville, Missouri, and had received a great deal of publicity around St. Louis. After the movie Ralph Walt asked Veleska, "What did you think of Belle Starr?" Veleska answered, "I liked her." "I'm glad," her father said, "for she was your great-grandmother." That was the first time Veleska knew of her Starr ancestry and has had an avid interest in her family history since.

JENNETTE STEELE ANDREWS

Jennette would have been around 19 at the time her mother, Pearl Starr, took her to Arizona. Apparently following her mother's teenage footsteps, Jennette became pregnant before leaving Fort Smith and Winslow. The father was said to have been a grocery boy. A daughter, Delores, was born from this early encounter. As Belle Starr had become violent over Pearl's first pregnancy, so did Pearl when she learned of Jennette's condition. Delores was given to an orphanage where she was raised. Later in life Jennette sent for the girl who joined her in Elko, Nevada. Delores is married and still resides there.

Going to Arizona with Pearl, Jennette later married an Indian by the name of Date Graham and is believed to have had a child by him. Nothing more is known of this early marriage or a possible child. An old cowboy in Elko, Nevada, who had been a close friend of Jennette's, told this writer of Jennette once mentioning this to him. A search for a Date Graham or their possible child has been fruitless to date. Veleska Ridley recalls that Graham was present when she visited Pearl and Jennette in Bisbee, Arizona as a child.

Why Jennette chose to go to Elko, Nevada is not known. There she met and married Hugh Farr. Farr, along with Leonard Slye, who later became Western movie star Roy Rogers, were original members of the Sons of the Pioneers singing group. According to Dale Warren, who has been with the Sons of the Pioneers for thirty-three years, the group often played in the Stockman Hotel there.

Farr, who was described as very quick tempered, was apparently only married to Jennette for a short time. Divorcing Farr, Jennette chose to enter the business her mother, Pearl, had been so successful in. Associated with a sporting house known as the Lucky Strike for a number of years, Jennette became quite popular with all the cowhands of the region. As one old cowboy, Walt James, recalled, everyone loved Jennette. "She not only provided a good place to have some fun after a hard week's work on the ranch, but provided us all with free counseling services. . . . Jennette took a real interest in all her friends' problems, and she helped us all better understand and work out our problems."

Jennette met a former ranch foreman, Ken Scott, in Elko and married him in 1938. The Scotts acquired both the Overland and Pioneer hotels there and operated gambling casinos. Jennette's half-sister, Ruth Robinson, later settled in Elko where she became a popular entertainer in the Scotts' hotels and casinos.

Kenneth Scott, who was still living in Elko when this writer visited there in October 1986, was also a writer.

Scott has published several books, and he and Jennette collaborated on a book about Jennette's grandmother entitled, *Belle Starr In Velvet*.

Jennette died in Elko on October 2, 1971. She was 68. Her only known child, Delores, still resides there and has no known descendents.

The two Starrs and the exciting lives they led during turbulent eras in American history will be long remembered by their descendents and in the annals of American history and folklore.

Charles Hutton and Flossie Pearl Hutton with son, Robert E. Hutton. Flossie was the daughter of Pearl Starr and Robert McClure.

Bibliography

BOOKS

Gaddy, Jerry. *Dust to Dust*. San Francisco: Presidio Press, 1979.

Hicks, Ed. *Belle Starr and her Pearl*. Little Rock: C. Armitage Harper Pioneer Press, 1963.

Mooney, Charles. *Doctor in Belle Starr Country*. Oklahoma City: Century Press, 1975.

Shackleford, William Yancey. *Belle Starr the Bandit Queen*. Girard, Kansas: Haldeman-Julius Publications, 1943.

Shirley, Glenn. *Belle Starr and her Times*. Norman: University of Oklahoma Press, 1982.

Winn, Robert G. *Two Starrs*. Fayetteville: Washington County Historical Society Publications, 1979.

PERIODICALS

Northeastern Nevada Historical Society Quarterly, Spring 1985.
Stearns Magazine, Oklahoma City.
Frontier Times, April 1936.

LETTERS

Belle Starr to Pearl Younger, February 1883.
Flossie Pearl Hutton to Robert Hutton, ca. 1924.
Flossie Pearl Hutton to Wichita newspaper, ca. 1924.
Brookie Craig to Author, 1987.
Kenneth Butler to Author, 1986, 1987.
Barbara Dew to Author, 1986.
Veleska Ridley to Author, 1987.
Flossie Wiley to Author, 1986, 1987.

Ozie Payne to Robert Winn, 1987.
Phillip Earl to Author, 1986, 1987.
Eunice Kelsey to Author, 1986.
Robert Hutton to Flossie Wiley, 1972.
Walt James to Author, 1984.
Nepanee Goforth to Author, 1987.
Pearl Starr to Flossie Epple Hutton (two letters), 1924.
Belle Starr to Marion Reed, 1871, 1872.

INTERVIEWS

Flossie Wiley, Colorado Springs, Colorado, 1986, 1987.
Veleska Myra Ridley, St. Louis, Missouri, 1987
Beth Greswold, Elko, Nevada, 1986.
Walt James, Elko, Nevada, 1986.
A.R. "Shorty" Miglioretto, Elko, Nevada, 1986.
Dotty Weeks, Elko, Nevada, 1986.
Tony Primeaux, Elko, Nevada, 1986.
Edna Patterson, Elko, Nevada, 1986.
Ray Hanley, Elko, Nevada, 1986.
Guy Nichols, Fort Smith, Arkansas, 1987.
Fadjo Cravens, Fort Smith, Arkansas, 1987.
Nepanee Goforth, Siloam Springs, Arkansas.
Lonnie Shannon, Cane Hill Arkansas, 1987.
Dale Warren (Sons of the Pioneers), 1987.

GOVERNMENT DOCUMENTS

U.S. Census Records (1850, 1860, 1870).
Marriage Records, Labette County, Kansas (1880)
Cherokee Tribal Marriage Records (1880).
Federal Court Records, Western District of Arkansas (1875–1894).
Circuit Court Records, Fayetteville, Arkansas (1911).
Bureau of Vital Statistics, Phoenix, Arizona (ca. 1925).
Marriage Records, Washington County, Arkansas (1897, 1902).
Court Records, Dallas County, Texas (1875, 1876).

NEWSPAPERS

St. Louis *Post-Dispatch*, 1929.
Fort Smith *Weekly Elevator*, 1886–1914.
Ottawa (Kansas) *Herald,* June 1978.
Elko *Free Press*, October 1971.
Dallas *Morning News* (1872–1876).

OTHER RESEARCH SOURCES

Oklahoma Historical Society, Oklahoma City, Oklahoma.
Nevada Historical Society, Reno, Nevada.
Northeastern Nevada Museum Library, Elko, Nevada.
Northeastern Historical Society, Reno, Nevada.
Elko Public Library, Elko, Nevada.
Washington County Historical Society, Fayetteville, Arkansas.
Burns Funeral Home, Elko, Nevada.
Brown and Page Funeral Home, Douglas, Arizona.
Ottawa Public Library, Ottawa, Kansas.
Fort Smith Historical Society, Fort Smith, Arkansas.
Charles M. Hiner: Grandson of Hiner & Hiner law firm in Fort Smith, Arkansas which represented both Belle and Pearl Starr in several cases.
Ross Pendergraft, Donrey Media Group.
Flossie Pearl Epple's research files and family history collections.
Judge Parker's Court, Fort Smith National Historic Site, Fort Smith, Arkansas.

Flossie Mae Wiley (center) with granddaughter, Lauralee Good, and husband Jack O. Wiley (right) during a 1987 visit to Fort Smith. Author Phillip Steele is at left.

FAMILY TREE

SAMUEL SHIRLEY
(?—1842)

JOHN SHIRLEY
(1794—1876)

JOHN SHIRLEY

PRESTON SHIRLEY
(1826—?)

CHARLOTTE A. SHIRLEY
(1838—?)

JOHN ALLISON SHIRLEY
(1842—1864)

MYRA MAEBELLE SHIRLEY
(1848—1889)

EDWIN BENTON SHIRLEY
(1850—1866)

MANSFIELD SHIRLEY
(1852—1867)

CRAVENS SHIRLEY
(1858—?)

MYRA MAEBELLE SHIRLEY
(BELLE STARR)

ROSE PEARL REED
(1868—1925)

EDWIN "EDDIE" REED
(1871—1896)

ROSE PEARL REED
(PEARL STARR)

MAMIE (FLOSSIE PEARL EPPLE)
(1887—1943)

RUTH KAIGLER
(1894—1979)

E. ERBACH
(1898—1899)

JENNETTE STEELE ANDREWS
(1902—1971)

FLOSSIE PEARL EPPLE
(HUTTON)

ROBERT E. HUTTON
(1908—1978)

RUTH KAIGLER
(WALT)

VELESKA MYRA WALT
(born 1912)

JENNETTE STEELE ANDREWS
(SCOTT)

DELORES VIGNOLO
(born 1921)

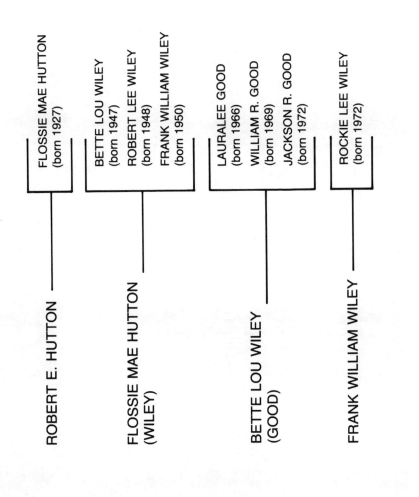

ROBERT E. HUTTON ——— FLOSSIE MAE HUTTON
(born 1927)

FLOSSIE MAE HUTTON
(WILEY)
BETTE LOU WILEY
(born 1947)
ROBERT LEE WILEY
(born 1948)
FRANK WILLIAM WILEY
(born 1950)

BETTE LOU WILEY
(GOOD)
LAURALEE GOOD
(born 1966)
WILLIAM R. GOOD
(born 1969)
JACKSON R. GOOD
(born 1972)

FRANK WILLIAM WILEY ——— ROCKIE LEE WILEY
(born 1972)

Ruth Kaigler Walt with daughter, Veleska Myra Walt. (Courtesy Veleska Ridley.)

Index